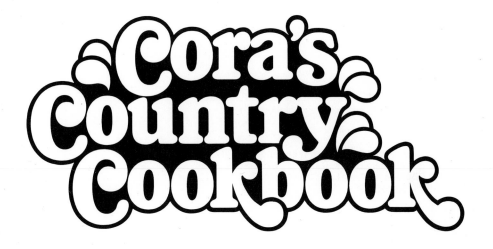

A Benjamin Company/Rutledge Book

MACMILLAN PUBLISHING CO., INC.

New York

COLLIER MACMILLAN PUBLISHERS

London

Library of Congress Cataloging in Publication Data

Cora.
  Cora's Country cookbook.
  "A Rutledge book."
  1. Cookery, American—New England.   I. Title.
II. Title: Country cookbook.
TX715.C794   641.5   77-6741
ISBN 0-02-528150-X

Color Photographs by Walter Storck

Prepared and produced by Rutledge Books,
a division of Arcata Consumer Products Corporation.
Published by:
  Macmillan Publishing Co., Inc.
  866 Third Avenue, New York, N.Y. 10022
  Collier Macmillan Canada, Ltd.
Printed in the United States of America
First Printing 1977

*Angel Flake, Baker's, Birds Eye, Calumet, Certo, Electra-Perk,
German's, Grape-Nuts, Jell-O, Log Cabin, Maxwell House, Minute and
Post are registered trademarks of General Foods Corporation.*

Contents

Cora says:

"Lots of folks say, 'Nothing good is ever easy.' Balderdash!! Everything's easy—once you know how to do it.

"Just sit yourself down and flip through my cookbook. No matter whether the recipe's old-fashioned or new-fashioned, you can always count on it being good!

"Cranberry muffins smothered in butter. Griddle cakes full of fresh plump blueberries. Roast pork with orange glaze. (Getting hungry?)

"Grandmother cooked like this *every day* of the week. No reason why you can't, too. You just gotta know how. And that's why I wrote this cookbook. Even slipped in some cooking tips to make it a might easier.

"What's my favorite recipe? I've got a sweet-tooth so I probably lean toward apple pie with a good steaming cup of coffee. But truth be known, I've always had a special hankering for pot roast.

"What's for dinner tonight? You decide. Just listen closely and you can make anything I can. And it'll always be good."

Cora

BRIGHTEN THE MORNING

Bring a little sunshine into the day! Start off right with an appetite-appealing bread or coffee cake. Or a batch of hot muffins—all so easy to make. If your homefolks don't cotton to getting up in the morning, the tempting smells will rouse even the most determined stay-in-beds. Make some coffee first thing, too. I don't think you can beat the smell of freshly brewed coffee for early-morning happiness. My recipes are also ideal for those weekend mornings when breakfast is later, when it slides into brunch-time. Then the pace is more leisurely. Whether you're serving a bona fide brunch to guests or a late family breakfast, these will hit the spot, get everyone off to a rousing beginning. Or think about weekday mid-morning kaffee-klatsches. Greet your friends with your own warm words of welcome—*and* the aromas of a delectable yeast bread and steaming coffee. Remember my homemade jams—they're an additional treat that perfectly complements these baked breakfast treats. Who said getting up in the morning was hard to take?

I call these my mainstays for the morning—the aromas make the day seem happy right away. Whether your taste runs to a quick hot bread, tasty muffins, coffee cake, sweet rolls or pancakes, you'll find a recipe to your liking here. But why choose? Try them all!

CEREAL BREAD

Cora says: "Cereal is the surprise ingredient here. It lends a rich, nutty taste to this unusual breakfast bread. Further bonus—you can make it the night before, slice it and heat or toast slices for breakfast."

1¾ cups all-purpose flour
1 cup sugar
2½ teaspoons Calumet baking powder
1 teaspoon salt
¾ cup Post Grape-Nuts brand cereal
1 cup milk
1 egg, well beaten
2 tablespoons shortening, melted

Mix flour with sugar, baking powder and salt. Stir in cereal. Blend milk with egg and shortening. Add flour mixture, stirring just until all flour is moistened. Pour into greased 9 × 5-inch loaf pan. Bake at 350° for 1 hour, or until cake tester inserted in center comes out clean. Cool in pan 10 minutes. Remove from pan and finish cooling on rack.

Note: For easier slicing, store bread overnight wrapped in wax paper, plastic wrap or aluminum foil.

Orange-Raisin Bread. Prepare Cereal Bread as directed, adding ½ cup raisins and ¼ cup grated orange rind with the cereal and substituting ½ cup orange juice for ½ cup of the milk. Bake about 1 hour and 5 minutes.

Banana Bread. Prepare Cereal Bread as directed, substituting 1 cup mashed banana for ½ cup of the milk. Bake about 1 hour and 5 minutes.

PANCAKE SPECIALS

Basic Recipe: Add 1 slightly beaten egg, 1¾ cups milk and 2 tablespoons liquid shortening to 2 cups pancake mix; beat until smooth. Bake on hot griddle, or in lightly greased skillet, turning to brown both sides. Serve with Log Cabin syrup. Makes about 20 four-inch pancakes.

Raisin Pancakes. Prepare pancakes as directed, adding ⅔ cup raisins to the batter.

Apple Pancakes. Prepare pancakes as directed, adding 1½ cups grated unpeeled apple, 2 tablespoons sugar and 2 teaspoons lemon juice to the batter.

Bacon Pancakes. Prepare pancakes as directed, adding 6 slices crisp bacon, crumbled, to the batter.

Orange Pancakes. Prepare pancakes as directed, reducing milk to ½ cup and adding 1¼ cups orange juice.

BLUEBERRY GRIDDLE CAKES

1¼ cups sifted all-purpose flour
2 tablespoons sugar
1½ teaspoons Calumet baking powder
¾ teaspoon salt
1 egg, well beaten
1 cup milk
3 tablespoons shortening, melted
1 to 1½ cups fresh blueberries
Log Cabin syrup

Sift flour with sugar, baking powder and salt. Combine egg, milk and shortening; add to flour mixture, mixing just until flour is dampened. (Batter will be lumpy.) Add berries. Bake on hot greased griddle. Serve with syrup, butter and grilled sausages, if desired. Makes 10 to 12 four-inch griddle cakes.

Note: Recipe may be doubled, using ⅓ cup melted shortening. For thinner griddle cakes, increase milk as desired.

Opposite: Blueberry Griddle Cakes

BRAN MUFFINS *(Illustrated page 33)*

⅔ cup all-purpose flour
2 tablespoons sugar
2½ teaspoons Calumet
    baking powder
¼ teaspoon salt
1 egg, beaten

¾ cup milk
3 tablespoons shortening,
    melted
1½ cups Post 40% bran
    flakes or Post raisin
    bran

Mix together flour, sugar, baking powder and salt. Combine egg and milk, add to flour mixture; then add shortening and mix only enough to dampen flour. Fold in cereal. Fill greased muffin pans two-thirds full. Bake at 425° for 15 to 20 minutes, or until golden brown. Makes 8 medium muffins.

Cranberry Bran Muffins. Sprinkle ½ cup chopped raw cranberries with 2 tablespoons sugar. Prepare Bran Muffins as directed, decreasing milk to ⅔ cup and adding the sweetened cranberries to batter with the cereal.

Molasses Bran Muffins. Prepare Bran Muffins as directed, decreasing milk to ⅔ cup and omitting the sugar. Combine ¼ cup molasses with milk before adding to batter.

CRANBERRY MUFFINS

Cora says: "Tart cranberries add wake-up flavor to these family-pleasing muffins."

1¾ cups all-purpose flour
2 tablespoons sugar
2½ teaspoons Calumet
    baking powder
¾ teaspoon salt
1 egg, well beaten

¾ cup milk
⅓ cup liquid shortening
1 cup chopped raw
    cranberries
3 tablespoons sugar

Mix flour with 2 tablespoons sugar, the baking powder and salt. Combine egg and milk and add all at once to flour mixture. Add shortening, and stir *only* until dry ingredients are dampened. (Batter will be lumpy.) Sprinkle cranberries with 3 tablespoons sugar and stir into batter. Spoon into greased muffin pans, filling each about two-thirds full. Bake at 400° for 25 to 30 minutes, or until done. Makes 10 muffins.

OLD-FASHIONED DOUGHNUTS

Cora says: "Much quicker to make than yeast-raised doughnuts, these deep-fried tidbits are good for breakfast, snack-time, any time!"

2 cups all-purpose flour	2 eggs, beaten
4 teaspoons Calumet baking powder	1 cup milk
1 tablespoon sugar	Confectioners sugar

Mix flour with baking powder and sugar. Combine eggs and milk. Add to flour mixture, mixing well; then beat until batter is smooth. Drop by teaspoonfuls into 1½ inches hot (375°) fat in deep saucepan. Fry 3 to 5 minutes, until golden brown, turning once. Drain on absorbent paper. Sprinkle with confectioners sugar. Makes about 4 dozen.

CINNAMON-APPLE COFFEE CAKE

Cora says: "This coffee cake gives you all the flavor of an apple pie—without the bother of making a crust."

2 cups all-purpose flour	3 medium apples, peeled and thinly sliced
⅓ cup sugar	
2½ teaspoons Calumet baking powder	2 tablespoons butter or margarine
¾ teaspoon salt	½ cup sugar
⅓ cup butter or other shortening	1 teaspoon ground cinnamon
⅔ cup milk	

Mix flour with ⅓ cup sugar, the baking powder and salt in a bowl. Cut in butter. Add milk all at once; stir carefully until all flour is dampened. Then stir vigorously until mixture forms a soft dough. Pat into a greased 8-inch square pan. Cover surface of dough with overlapping apple slices and dot with butter. Combine ½ cup sugar and the cinnamon; sprinkle over apples. Bake at 375° for 40 to 45 minutes, or until cake tester inserted in center comes out clean. Cut in squares and serve warm with cream, if desired.

SWEET YEAST DOUGH

Cora says: "This dough is the basis for the three delicious recipes that follow. Sprinkle it with your favorite crumb topping or glaze it with a confectioners sugar icing."

2 packages active dry yeast
½ cup warm (not hot) water
¾ cup lukewarm milk
1 cup butter or margarine, melted and cooled
2 eggs, beaten
¼ cup sugar
1 teaspoon salt
1 teaspoon grated lemon rind
4½ cups (about) all-purpose flour

Dissolve yeast in warm water; combine with remaining ingredients in a large bowl. Beat until smooth, about 1 minute. (Dough will be very soft.) Cover with a damp cloth. Place in refrigerator for at least 2 hours or overnight. Shape as desired. Makes enough dough for 18 buns, 24 large or 36 small rolls, 2 braided coffee cakes, or 1 larger coffee cake.

CINNAMON-RAISIN BUNS

Sweet Yeast Dough (above)
Melted butter or margarine
1 cup sugar
⅔ cup raisins
2 teaspoons ground cinnamon

Divide dough in half. Roll each half into a 14 × 9-inch rectangle and brush lightly with melted butter. Combine sugar, raisins and cinnamon; sprinkle over dough. Roll as for a jelly roll, starting at short side. Cut each roll into 9 equal pieces. Place, cut side up, about 1 inch apart in 2 greased 9-inch layer pans or 8-inch square pans. Cover with clean towel and let rise in warm place, free from draft, until doubled in bulk, about 1 hour. Bake at 350° for about 35 minutes, or until lightly browned. Drizzle Confectioners Sugar Glaze over top, if desired. Makes 18 buns.

Confectioners Sugar Glaze. Add 1 tablespoon (about) hot milk or water to 1 cup sifted confectioners sugar in a bowl; blend well. Makes ⅓ cup.

Opposite: Coffee Twists (front; recipe, p. 14), Date-Nut Coffee Cake (left; recipe, p. 15), and Cinnamon Raisin Buns (right)—all made with Sweet Yeast Dough

COFFEE TWISTS *(Illustrated page 12)*

Cora says: "One of my favorites—a real pick-me-up with that mid-morning cup of coffee!"

½ cup butter or margarine
⅔ cup firmly packed brown sugar
2 teaspoons corn syrup
¾ cup chopped pecans
Sweet Yeast Dough (see page 13)

¼ cup butter or margarine, melted
½ cup firmly packed brown sugar
2 teaspoons ground cinnamon

Melt ½ cup butter in saucepan. Add ⅔ cup brown sugar and the corn syrup. Bring to a full rolling boil, and pour immediately into two 15 × 10-inch pans. Sprinkle with nuts.

Divide dough in half. Roll each half into a 12-inch square and brush with 2 tablespoons of the melted butter. Combine ½ cup brown sugar and the cinnamon; sprinkle 2 tablespoons of the brown sugar mixture in a strip down the center of each square. Fold one-third of the dough over the centers; sprinkle with remaining brown sugar mixture. Fold remaining third over the two layers. Cut with sharp knife crosswise into strips, ½ to 1 inch wide. Hold strips at each end, twist in opposite directions, and seal ends well. Place in pans, about 1½ inches apart. Cover with a clean towel, and let rise in warm place, free from draft, until doubled in bulk, about 1 hour. Bake at 400° for about 20 minutes. Invert pan onto cake rack at once. Serve warm. Makes 48 small or 24 large rolls.

DATE-NUT COFFEE CAKE *(Illustrated page 12)*

Cora says: "A luscious filling makes this fancy-looking coffee cake extra special."

1 cup chopped pitted dates
⅔ cup water
½ cup chopped nuts
¼ cup firmly packed brown
    sugar
1 tablespoon lemon juice
    Sweet Yeast Dough (see
    page 13)
1 egg yolk

2 tablespoons milk
⅓ cup all-purpose flour
2 tablespoons granulated
    sugar
2 tablespoons butter or
    margarine
½ teaspoon ground
    cinnamon

Combine dates, water, nuts, brown sugar and lemon juice in a saucepan. Bring to a boil over medium heat, stirring constantly, and continue boiling until mixture is thickened. Cool.

Divide dough in half. Roll each half into a 16 × 8-inch rectangle. Spread half the date filling down center third of each rectangle. Cut 15 slits in dough along each side of filling, making strips about 1 inch wide. Fold strips at an angle across filling, alternating from side to side. Place on greased baking sheet. If desired, form into a ring; placing one end in the other and sealing together firmly. Cover and let rise in warm place, free from draft, until doubled in bulk.

Combine egg yolk and milk; brush over cakes. Combine flour, sugar, butter and cinnamon. Sprinkle half of mixture on each cake. Bake at 350° for about 30 minutes, or until lightly browned.

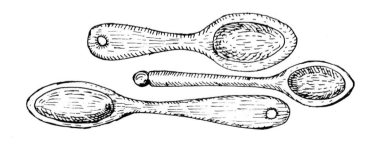

HONEY-COCONUT SWEET ROLLS

Cora says: "Here's a nice change from pecan sticky buns —orange rind and coconut make these rolls downright ambrosial!"

3 cups sifted all-purpose flour	1½ teaspoons ground cinnamon
⅓ cup sugar	¾ teaspoon grated orange rind
3¾ teaspoons Calumet baking powder	½ teaspoon salt
1 teaspoon salt	⅓ cup honey
½ cup shortening	2½ tablespoons butter or margarine, softened
1 cup milk	¾ cup Baker's Angel Flake coconut
1 egg, beaten	
⅓ cup firmly packed brown sugar	

Sift flour with sugar, baking powder and 1 teaspoon salt. Cut in shortening. Combine milk and egg and add to flour mixture. Stir with fork until soft dough is formed. Turn out on a lightly floured board and knead 30 seconds. Roll into a 15 × 10-inch rectangle, ¼ inch thick.

Combine brown sugar, cinnamon, orange rind and ½ teaspoon salt; blend in honey and butter. Spread half of the mixture on dough and sprinkle with half of the coconut. Roll as for jelly roll and cut in 1-inch slices. Arrange cut side down in lightly greased muffin pans. Spread top with remaining brown sugar mixture and sprinkle with remaining coconut. Bake at 425° for 20 minutes, or until golden brown. Makes 15 rolls.

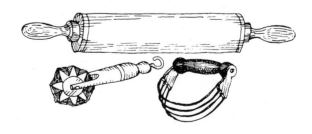

These accompaniments will set off whatever else you're having for breakfast. The jams are my "dividends"—made when I had the time, held in reserve to be enjoyed whenever I like. Jams, marmalades, a conserve—great on toast or muffins. Or have my Maple-Flavored Cranberry Sauce (page 20) on pancakes or waffles—deliciously different!

CITRUS MARMALADE

Cora says: "The addition of lemons gives this marmalade a delicious two-fruit flavor."

3 cups prepared fruit*   ½ bottle Certo fruit pectin
5 cups (2¼ lb.) sugar

3 medium oranges, 2 medium lemons, 1½ cups water and ⅛ teaspoon baking soda

First prepare the fruit. Section 3 oranges and 2 lemons, reserving the rinds and any juice. Dice the fruit and set aside. Trim about half the white membrane from the rinds; cut into thin slivers, or chop or grind. Combine 1½ cups water, ⅛ teaspoon baking soda and the rinds in a saucepan. Bring to a boil; cover and simmer 20 minutes, stirring occasionally. Add reserved fruit and juice, and simmer 10 minutes longer. Measure 3 cups into a *large* saucepan.

Then make the marmalade. Thoroughly mix sugar into fruit in saucepan. Place over high heat, bring to a *full rolling boil* and *boil hard 1 minute*, stirring constantly. Remove from heat and at once stir in fruit pectin. Skim off foam with metal spoon. Then stir and skim for 7 minutes to cool slightly and prevent floating fruit. Ladle quickly into glasses. Cover at once with ⅛-inch hot paraffin. Makes 5½ cups or about 7 (6 fl. oz.) glasses.

PEACH-PINEAPPLE CONSERVE

2¼ cups prepared fruit*
½ cup drained maraschino cherries
¼ cup lemon juice (2 lemons)

1 can (8 oz.) crushed pineapple
1½ cups chopped nuts
7½ cups (3¼ lb.) sugar
1 bottle Certo fruit pectin

*about 2½ lb. fully ripe peaches

First prepare the fruit. Peel and pit about 2½ pounds peaches. Grind or chop very fine. Measure 2¼ cups into a *large* saucepan. Finely chop ½ cup maraschino cherries. Squeeze juice from 2 lemons; measure ¼ cup. Add cherries, lemon juice and pineapple to peaches.

Then make the conserve. Thoroughly mix nuts and sugar into fruit in saucepan. Place over high heat, bring to a *full rolling boil* and *boil hard 1 minute*, stirring constantly. Remove from heat and at once stir in fruit pectin. Skim off foam with metal spoon. Then stir and skim for 5 minutes to cool slightly and prevent floating fruit. Ladle quickly into glasses. Cover at once with ⅛-inch hot paraffin. Makes 8¾ cups or about 11 (6 fl. oz.) glasses.

CHERRY JAM

4 cups prepared fruit*
7 cups (3 lb.) sugar

1 bottle Certo fruit pectin

*about 3 lb. fully ripe sour cherries

First prepare the fruit. Stem and pit about 3 pounds sour cherries and chop fine. Measure 4 cups into a *large* saucepan.

Then make the jam. Thoroughly mix sugar into fruit in saucepan. Place over high heat, bring to a *full rolling boil* and *boil hard 1 minute,* stirring constantly. Remove from heat and at once stir in fruit pectin. Skim off foam with metal spoon. Then stir and skim for 5 minutes to cool slightly and prevent floating fruit. Ladle quickly into glasses. Cover at once with ⅛-inch hot paraffin. Makes 8¾ cups or about 11 (6 fl. oz.) glasses.

Note: For a stronger cherry flavor, add ¼ teaspoon almond extract to prepared jam just before ladling into glasses.

BLUEBERRY JAM

Cora says: "Tied with pretty ribbon, jars of this tasty jam make welcome gifts."

2½ cups prepared fruit*
  2 tablespoons lemon juice
    (1 lemon)

4 cups (1¾ lb.) sugar
½ bottle Certo fruit pectin

*about 1 qt. fully ripe blueberries

First prepare the fruit. Thoroughly crush about 1 quart fully ripe blueberries. Measure 2½ cups into a *large* saucepan. Squeeze the juice from 1 lemon; add 2 tablespoons to fruit.

Then make the jam. Thoroughly mix sugar into fruit in saucepan. Place over high heat, bring to a *full rolling boil* and *boil hard 1 minute,* stirring constantly. Remove from heat and at once stir in fruit pectin. Skim off foam with metal spoon. Then stir and skim for 5 minutes to cool slightly and prevent floating fruit. Ladle quickly into glasses. Cover at once with ⅛-inch hot paraffin. Makes about 4 cups or 6 (6 fl. oz.) glasses.

STRAWBERRY JAM

Cora says: "When strawberries are in season, make a few batches of this recipe—you can bring the taste of summer to the dead of winter!"

4 cups prepared fruit*
7 cups (3 lb.) sugar

½ bottle Certo fruit pectin

*about 2 qt. fully ripe strawberries

First prepare the fruit. Stem and halve about 2 quarts strawberries; cut large berries in quarters. Measure 4 cups into a *very large* saucepan. Add 1 cup of the sugar, mix carefully and let stand 15 minutes.

Then make the jam. Carefully but thoroughly mix remaining 6 cups sugar into fruit in saucepan. Place over high heat, bring to a *full rolling boil* and *boil hard 1 minute,* stirring constantly. Remove from heat and at once stir in fruit pectin. Skim off foam with metal spoon. Then stir and skim for 5 minutes to cool slightly and prevent floating fruit. Ladle quickly into glasses. Cover at once with ⅛-inch hot paraffin. Makes about 8 cups or 10 (6 fl. oz.) glasses.

CARROT MARMALADE

Cora says: "The addition of cinnamon or ginger makes this unusual marmalade a good go-along with roast meat. Try it with my Orange-Glazed Roast Pork (page 61)."

4 cups prepared carrot and
fruit mixture*
2 to 3 teaspoons ground
cinnamon or ginger
(optional)

7 cups (3 lb.) sugar
½ bottle Certo fruit pectin

about 1½ lb. carrots, 2 medium oranges and 4 medium lemons

First prepare the carrot and fruit mixture. Cook about 1½ pounds carrots until tender, about 20 minutes; drain, and finely chop or grind. Grate the rind and dice the pulp from 2 oranges. Squeeze the juice from 4 lemons. Mix carrots with orange pulp, orange rind and lemon juice. Measure 4 cups into a *very large* saucepan.

Then make the marmalade. Thoroughly mix cinnamon and sugar into mixture in saucepan. Place over high heat, bring to a *full rolling boil* and *boil hard 1 minute,* stirring constantly. Remove from heat and at once stir in fruit pectin. Skim off foam with metal spoon. Then stir and skim for 5 minutes to cool slightly and prevent floating fruit. Ladle quickly into glasses. Cover at once with ⅛-inch hot paraffin. Makes about 8 cups or 10 (6 fl. oz.) glasses.

MAPLE-FLAVORED CRANBERRY SAUCE

Cora says: "I'm proud of this combination. Cranberries add just the right bite. Pancakes never had it so good!"

1½ cups Log Cabin syrup
½ cup water

1 pound (4 cups) fresh
cranberries

Combine syrup and water in a 2-quart saucepan; add cranberries. Bring to a boil and cook, uncovered, for 5 minutes, without stirring. Remove from heat; cover and let stand 5 minutes. Return to heat; cover and cook 5 minutes longer. Cool without stirring, then chill. Makes 3½ cups.

MIDDAY CHEER

"I'm starved!" Sound familiar? Lunchtime already, and it's a question of what to fix. You want variety from day to day, and it's only too easy to find yourself serving the same old-standby lunches. Branch out a bit—think of different combinations. These soup and salad recipes in combination with favorite sandwiches will pick up your family's lunchtime spirits—I practically guarantee it. To pick up spirits even further, serve mugs of coffee as a robust go-along—somehow coffee almost tastes different to me when I sip it from a thick earthenware mug. You can put together these lunches with a minimum of time and trouble. Your return? Maximum enjoyment. Try out mix-and-match ideas from these meal makers, depending on how light or hearty you want lunch to be. You can run the gamut here. For a small, quick-to-fix meal, why not have one of my rib-sticking soups along with an English muffin, then some fresh fruit for dessert? They're medium-hungry? Have a soup and salad, soup and sandwich, or salad and sandwich (maybe a few cookies, too). The choice is yours—flexibility is the key word here!

Warm-Welcome Soups and Chowders
These are cold-weather favorites, great for starting—or being—a meal on blustery winter days. But think of them for quick pickups mid-morning or mid-afternoon, too. When the weather is warm, I like to have the Potato and Leek Soup chilled. Very refreshing!

LENTIL SOUP

Cora says: "A stick-to-the-ribs soup."

1½ cups dried lentils	1 cup diced carrots
Water	2 whole cloves
4 ounces salt pork, cubed	2 bay leaves
1 cup chopped onions	2¼ teaspoons salt
½ garlic clove, chopped	Dash of pepper
4 cups beef stock	3 tablespoons cider vinegar
2 cups chopped celery	(optional)

Place lentils in large saucepan; add water to cover and let stand overnight. Drain, reserving liquid. Add water to liquid to make 6 cups. Heat salt pork in a skillet; add onions and garlic and sauté until onions are tender but not browned. Combine measured liquid, beef stock, celery, carrots, cloves, bay leaves, salt, pepper, the onion mixture and the lentils in a large heavy saucepan. Cover and simmer about 4 hours, or until lentils are soft. Add vinegar; remove bay leaves. Makes about 9 cups or 8 to 10 servings.

POTATO AND LEEK SOUP

Cora says: "This smooth but hearty soup is good hot or cold—it can warm frozen fingers and toes in the winter or revive wilted summer appetites."

8 medium potatoes, peeled and sliced (6 cups)	1 cup light cream or half and half
6 leeks or 3 medium onions, sliced (2 cups)	2 tablespoons butter or margarine
1½ quarts water	2 teaspoons salt
4 chicken bouillon cubes	Dash of pepper

Place potatoes and leeks in large saucepan. Add water and bouillon cubes. Simmer about 45 minutes, or until very soft. Press through sieve. Add cream, butter, salt and pepper, and heat. Makes 8½ cups or 8 servings.

Note: Soup may be chilled well and served cold; add additional light cream for a thinner consistency, if desired. Sprinkle with chopped chives or parsley.

CORN AND TOMATO CHOWDER

Cora says: "Easy and quick—filling, too, teamed with a hamburger or grilled cheese sandwich."

¼ cup chopped celery	1 can (16 oz.) tomatoes
2 tablespoons chopped onion	1¾ teaspoons salt
1 tablespoon chopped green pepper	1 teaspoon sugar
2 tablespoons shortening	¼ teaspoon baking soda
1 can (17 oz.) whole kernel corn	⅛ teaspoon pepper
	3 cups milk, scalded

Sauté celery, onion and green pepper in shortening in saucepan until golden brown. Add corn and tomatoes; simmer 5 minutes. Stir in salt, sugar, baking soda and pepper. Gradually stir corn mixture into scalded milk. Makes about 6 cups or 6 servings.

NEW ENGLAND CLAM CHOWDER
(Illustrated page 36)

3 medium potatoes, peeled and diced (about 1½ cups)
2 cups water
1 bottle (8 oz.) clam juice
1 can (10¾ oz.) condensed cream of celery soup
¾ cup milk
1 can (7½ oz.) minced clams
1 tablespoon butter or margarine
1 tablespoon chopped parsley
2 teaspoons lemon juice
1 teaspoon salt

Combine potatoes, water and clam juice in a large saucepan. Bring to a boil; reduce heat and cook until potatoes are tender, about 30 minutes. Add soup, milk, clams, butter, parsley, lemon juice and salt, and simmer gently about 10 minutes, stirring occasionally. Garnish with additional chopped parsley, if desired. Makes 6 cups or 6 servings.

Note: For slightly thicker soup, combine 1 tablespoon cornstarch and 2 tablespoons water; stir into soup and cook about 2 minutes longer.

VEGETABLE BEEF SOUP

1 pound ground beef
1 cup chopped onions
2 tablespoons butter or margarine
4 cups hot water
1 can (16 oz.) tomatoes
1 cup sliced celery
1 tablespoon salt
2 bouillon cubes
½ bay leaf
½ teaspoon Worcestershire sauce
⅛ teaspoon pepper
1 package (10 oz.) Birds Eye 5 minute mixed vegetables
1 cup egg noodles
½ teaspoon thyme

Sauté beef and onions in butter in large saucepan until meat is well browned. Add water, tomatoes, celery, salt, bouillon cubes, bay leaf, Worcestershire sauce and pepper. Bring to a boil; cover and simmer 30 minutes.

Add mixed vegetables, noodles and thyme. Bring to a boil. Cover and simmer 15 minutes. Makes about 9½ cups or 8 to 10 servings.

Opposite: Vegetable Beef Soup

Super-Good Salads

Main-dish salads, potato salad, molded salads—I've given you all of them. Naturally, these are good for dinner, too—or for picnics or buffets. I think you'll like the molded salads for dessert, too. Don't forget that all of these are easily made ahead of time—added solid comfort for those short-on-time days.

FROZEN FRUIT SALAD SUPREME

Cora says: "This is rich and delicious—it makes an appealing frosty dessert, good with home-baked cookies."

1 package (3 oz.) Jell-O brand lemon gelatin	2 cans (8¼ oz. each) crushed pineapple in syrup, drained
¼ teaspoon salt	
1 cup boiling water	1 cup diced bananas
½ cup orange juice	2 tablespoons diced maraschino cherries
2 tablespoons lemon juice	
¼ cup mayonnaise	¼ cups thinly sliced blanched almonds
½ cup heavy cream, whipped	

Dissolve gelatin and salt in boiling water. Add orange juice, lemon juice and mayonnaise, blending well. Chill until slightly thickened. Fold in whipped cream and the fruits and nuts. Pour into an 8- or 9-inch square pan. Freeze until firm, 3 to 4 hours. Thaw in refrigerator about 30 minutes before serving. Cut in slices or squares. Serve on crisp lettuce, plain or with mayonnaise, if desired. Makes about 4¼ cups or 8 servings.

CRANBERRY-PINEAPPLE MOLD

Cora says: "Pair this with a poultry main dish for an unusual taste treat."

1 can (8¼ oz.) crushed pineapple in syrup	1½ cups fresh cranberries, ground, or 1 can (8 oz.) whole berry cranberry sauce
1 package (3 oz.) Jell-O brand gelatin, any red flavor	
1 cup boiling water	½ cup finely diced celery

Drain pineapple, measuring syrup. Add water to syrup to make
½ cup. Dissolve gelatin in boiling water. Add measured liquid and cranberries. Chill until slightly thickened. Stir in pineapple and celery. Pour into 4-cup mold or individual molds. Chill until firm, about 3 hours. Unmold. Makes 3½ cups or 6 salad or 10 relish servings.

JELLIED WALDORF SALAD

Cora says: "Here's a variation on the famous Waldorf Salad—makes a delicious and attractive dessert, too."

1 package (3 oz.) Jell-O brand lemon gelatin	1½ cups diced unpeeled red apples
½ teaspoon salt	½ cup diced celery
1 cup boiling water	¼ cup chopped walnuts
¾ cup cold water	¼ cup mayonnaise (optional)
2 teaspoons vinegar	

Dissolve gelatin and salt in boiling water. Add cold water and vinegar. Chill until thickened. Fold in apples, celery, nuts and mayonnaise. Pour into a 4-cup mold or individual molds. Chill until firm, about 3 hours. Unmold. Serve with crisp greens and mayonnaise, if desired. Makes about 3 cups or 6 servings.

TURKEY SALAD

Cora says: "A main-dish salad is as good in the winter as it is in the summer. It's an ideal way to use leftover turkey and a welcome change from hot main dishes."

5 cups diced cooked turkey or chicken	1½ teaspoons salt
2½ cups diced celery	1 teaspoon grated onion
1¼ cups mayonnaise	½ teaspoon celery seed
¼ cup lemon juice	⅛ teaspoon pepper

Combine all ingredients in bowl and toss lightly to blend well. Chill at least 2 hours. Serve on crisp lettuce, if desired. Makes 6 cups or 8 servings.

THREE BEAN SALAD

1 package (9 oz.) Birds Eye 5 minute cut wax beans
1 package (9 oz.) Birds Eye 5 minute cut green beans
1 package (10 oz.) Birds Eye 5 minute baby lima beans
1½ cups salted water
½ cup vinegar
¼ cup water
¼ cup salad oil
3 tablespoons minced onion
2 tablespoons chopped pimiento
½ teaspoon salt
¼ teaspoon Worcestershire sauce
Dash of pepper

Prepare beans together in 1½ cups salted water as directed on packages; drain. Combine remaining ingredients; pour over beans. Chill at least 4 hours to marinate, stirring once or twice. Spoon into lettuce-lined bowl. Makes about 4 cups or 4 entrée salads.

POTATO SALAD SUPREME

Cora says: "The secret to its great flavor is combining the seasonings with the potatoes while they are still warm."

7 cups warm sliced boiled potatoes
⅓ cup chopped chives
¼ cup salad oil
¼ cup vinegar
1 tablespoon grated onion
1 teaspoon salt
⅛ teaspoon pepper
¾ cup sour cream
¾ cup mayonnaise
½ cup chopped celery
½ cup diced cucumber

Combine potatoes, chives, oil, vinegar, onion, salt and pepper; toss well and chill. Meanwhile, combine sour cream, mayonnaise, celery and cucumber, and chill. Just before serving, add mayonnaise mixture to potato mixture, mixing well. Garnish with cherry tomatoes, or serve with lettuce and sliced hard-cooked eggs or tomato wedges, if desired. Makes about 8 cups or 8 servings.

Opposite: Three Bean Salad (front), Potato Salad Supreme (left), and Spiced Jellied Peaches (right; recipe, p. 30)

SPICED JELLIED PEACHES
(Illustrated page 28)

1 can (17 oz.) sliced peaches
¾ cup cold water
2 tablespoons vinegar
12 whole cloves
1 cinnamon stick
1 package (3 oz.) Jell-O brand orange gelatin

Drain peaches, measuring syrup. Add water to syrup to make 1 cup. Dice the peaches. Combine measured liquid, the water, vinegar and spices in a saucepan. Bring to a boil; reduce heat and simmer 10 minutes. Strain, discarding spices. Dissolve gelatin in hot liquid. Chill until slightly thickened. Stir in peaches and pour into individual molds. Chill until firm, about 3 hours. Unmold. Garnish with salad greens, if desired. Makes 3 cups or 6 servings.

Note: Recipe may be doubled, reducing cold water to 1 cup; chill overnight in a tall 6-cup mold.

COLESLAW COOLER

Cora says: "Here's a delicious variation for those who love coleslaw."

1 package (3 oz.) Jell-O brand orange-pineapple or lemon gelatin
½ teaspoon salt
1 cup boiling water
½ cup cold water
2 tablespoons vinegar
½ cup mayonnaise
½ cup sour cream
1 tablespoon prepared mustard
1 teaspoon grated onion
3 cups shredded cabbage
2 tablespoons diced pimiento
1 tablespoon chopped parsley

Dissolve gelatin and salt in boiling water. Add cold water and vinegar. Stir in mayonnaise, sour cream, mustard and onion, blending thoroughly. Chill until thickened. Fold in cabbage, pimiento and parsley. Pour into a 4-cup mold or serving bowl. Chill until firm, about 3 hours. Makes 4 cups or 6 to 8 servings.

CUCUMBER-SOUR CREAM MOLD

2 medium cucumbers,
peeled and coarsely
grated (about 1½
cups)
1 package (3 oz.) Jell-O
brand lemon or lime
gelatin
1 teaspoon salt
1 cup boiling water

¾ cup cold water
2 teaspoons vinegar
½ cup sour cream
1 tablespoon chopped
onion
1 tablespoon chopped
parsley
⅛ teaspoon coarsely
ground black pepper

Wrap grated cucumbers in a clean cloth and squeeze tightly to remove liquid; drain. Dissolve gelatin and salt in boiling water. Add cold water and vinegar. Blend in sour cream. Chill until thickened. Fold in drained cucumbers, onion, parsley and pepper. Pour into individual molds or a 4-cup mold. Chill until firm, about 4 hours. Unmold. Serve with meat or seafood. Makes about 3⅔ cups or 6 servings.

SEAFOOD-STUFFED TOMATOES

(Illustrated page 33)

Cora says: "The filling makes a perfect stuffing for avocados, too—or use it as a sandwich filling, on bread spread with mayonnaise or salad dressing."

4 large tomatoes
1 can (9¼ oz.) tuna (or
shrimp, crab meat,
lobster), drained and
flaked

⅓ cup finely chopped
celery
2 hard-cooked eggs,
chopped

Cut out stem end of tomatoes. Then cut each into 6 wedges, cutting to within ¼ inch of bottom. Combine tuna, celery and eggs. Spread tomato wedges apart and spoon tuna mixture into center, allowing about ½ cup each. Serve on salad greens with dressing, if desired. Makes 4 servings.

Note: Tomatoes may be peeled, if desired.

Round out your lunch with one of these—home-baked rolls or a tangy relish can make all the difference in the world. These small but satisfying additions will help lift any meal out of the ordinary.

REFRIGERATOR ROLL DOUGH

Cora says: "Mmmm—the smell of yeast dough baking. Heartwarming and soul-warming—says you really care to the family."

¾ cup hot water
½ cup sugar
1 tablespoon salt
¼ cup shortening
2 packages active dry yeast

1 cup warm (not hot) water
1 egg, beaten
5¼ cups (about) sifted all-purpose flour

Combine hot water, sugar, salt and shortening. Cool to lukewarm. Sprinkle yeast over warm water in a large mixing bowl; stir until dissolved. Stir in lukewarm water mixture. Add egg and 2½ cups of the flour; beat until smooth. Stir in remaining flour and beat 1 minute. Dough will be soft. Place dough in greased bowl; brush top with soft shortening. Cover tightly with wax paper or aluminum foil. Store in refrigerator until doubled in bulk. (Dough may be kept 1 week in refrigerator, at about 40° to 45°.)

Pan Rolls. Divide dough in half. Form each half into a roll about 12 inches long and cut each roll into 16 equal pieces. Form each piece into a smooth ball and place in 2 greased 8-inch layer or square pans, about ¼ inch apart. Cover and let rise in warm place, free from draft, until doubled in bulk, about 1 hour. Brush lightly with melted butter or margarine. Bake at 375° for about 20 minutes. Makes 32 rolls.

Opposite: Seafood-Stuffed Tomatoes (recipe, p. 31) and Bran Muffins (recipe, p. 10)

CORN RELISH

Cora says: "Makes even a plain hamburger something to sit up and cheer about—when it's served with this tangy homemade relish."

½ cup chopped onion
⅓ cup vinegar
¼ cup chopped green
    pepper
3 tablespoons sugar
2 tablespoons chopped red
    pepper or pimiento

¾ teaspoon salt
½ teaspoon celery seed
½ teaspoon dry mustard
1 package (10 oz.) Birds
    Eye 5 minute sweet
    whole kernel corn

Combine all ingredients except corn in saucepan. Bring to a boil. Reduce heat; cover and simmer 12 minutes, stirring occasionally. Add corn and bring again to a boil. Reduce heat; cover and simmer 5 minutes, or until corn is just tender. Serve hot or cold. Makes 2 cups.

BOSTON BROWN BREAD
(Illustrated page 36)

Cora says: "This traditionally accompanies New England Baked Beans (page 81), but it's equally good sliced and toasted, then spread with butter—maybe for breakfast or your afternoon coffee break."

1 cup rye flour
1 cup whole wheat flour
1 cup cornmeal
1½ teaspoons baking soda
1 teaspoon salt

2 cups buttermilk or sour
    milk
¾ cup dark molasses
¾ cup raisins (optional)

Combine rye flour, whole wheat flour, cornmeal, soda and salt. Mix milk and molasses, blending well. Add flour mixture gradually, beating well after each addition. Stir in raisins. Pour into 2 well-greased 8 × 4-inch loaf pans or 1-quart molds. Cover pans loosely with buttered wax paper, then with aluminum foil, and tie securely with string. Place on rack in a large deep saucepan; add boiling water to reach halfway up sides of pans.

Cover and simmer 2 hours, or until tester inserted in center comes out almost clean. Remove from saucepan, remove foil and wax paper, then remove from pans and cool on racks.

HERB JELLY

Cora says: "I like this with most any roast meat sandwich —try it with lamb as a change from the usual mint jelly. It's a great addition to a dinner menu, as well."

2 cups herb infusion*	Few drops green food
4½ cups (2 lb.) sugar	coloring
¼ cup vinegar	½ bottle Certo fruit pectin

2½ cups boiling water and 4 tablespoons dried herb leaves—sage, thyme, tarragon or marjoram leaves, or a combination

First prepare the herb infusion. Pour 2½ cups boiling water over 4 tablespoons herb leaves. Cover and let stand 15 minutes. Strain through cheesecloth or jelly bag; measure 2 cups into a *large* saucepan.

Then make the jelly. Thoroughly mix sugar and vinegar into infusion in saucepan. Place over high heat and bring to a boil, stirring constantly. Add food coloring. At once stir in fruit pectin. Then bring to a *full rolling boil* and *boil hard 1 minute*, stirring constantly. Remove from heat, skim off foam with metal spoon and pour quickly into glasses. Cover at once with ⅛ inch hot paraffin. Makes 4½ cups or 6 (6 fl. oz.) glasses.

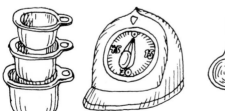

AFTERNOON REFRESHMENT —THE COFFEE BREAK

Baked goodies that warm the heart as they warm the inner man or woman—what could be better with that warming cup of afternoon coffee? We all need to take a break occasionally, put our feet up and relax with friends. Nothing makes people feel more at home, more comfortable, than some homemade treats like these when they drop by. Make sure you have a big pot of rich, full-flavored coffee, too—no smell in the world is friendlier, says "Welcome!" louder. Taste is pretty hard to resist, too. And I haven't met anyone yet who could resist a handful of my cookies or a few slices of a sweet bread come mid-afternoon. Offering one of these just seems like the neighborly thing to do, gives me an opportunity to get to know people a little better. Amazing—after you sit and visit over an afternoon, you find that you're refreshed, too. And I've found out something else. Aside from being great to serve to guests, most of these cookies and sweet breads make thoughtful gifts. Unexpected gifts can be the most heartwarming of all—when they come from the heart of the giver.

Opposite: New England Clam Chowder (recipe, p. 24) and Boston Brown Bread (recipe, p. 34)

Cookies and Small Cakes

Whenever you have an energy letdown, it might be an idea to think of a few cookies. Between lunch and dinner time, I feel the need of a little something, and these do fill the bill. Delightful to serve with sit-down coffee, they're mighty welcome in a lunch box, too.

BROWNIES

Cora says: "Moist and chewy or cake-like—whichever you vote for—brownies have to rank high on nearly everyone's list of favorite sweets."

2 squares Baker's unsweetened chocolate
⅓ cup soft butter or other shortening
⅔ cup all-purpose flour
½ teaspoon Calumet baking powder
¼ teaspoon salt
2 eggs
1 cup sugar
1 teaspoon vanilla
½ cup chopped nuts

Melt chocolate with butter over low heat. Mix flour with baking powder and salt. Beat eggs well; then gradually beat in sugar. Beat in chocolate mixture and vanilla. Add flour mixture and mix well. Stir in nuts. Spread in greased 8-inch square pan. Bake at 350° for 25 minutes (for moist chewy brownies) or about 30 minutes or until cake tester inserted in center comes out clean (for cake-like brownies). Cool in pan; then cut into squares or rectangles. Makes about 20 brownies.

Note: This recipe may be doubled and baked in a greased 13 × 9-inch pan at 350° for 25 to 30 minutes as directed. Makes about 40 brownies.

HONEY FUDGE BROWNIES

⅔ cup sifted all-purpose flour
½ teaspoon Calumet baking powder
¼ teaspoon salt
⅓ cup butter or other shortening
2 squares Baker's unsweetened chocolate

¾ cup sugar*
2 eggs, well beaten
¼ cup honey*
½ cup chopped walnuts
1 teaspoon vanilla

*or ½ cup sugar and ½ cup honey

Sift flour with baking powder and salt. Melt butter and chocolate in saucepan over low heat. Add sugar gradually to eggs, beating thoroughly. Add honey and chocolate mixture; blend well. Add flour mixture and mix thoroughly. Add nuts and vanilla and pour into a greased 8-inch square pan. Bake at 350° for 30 to 35 minutes. Cool in pan. Cut into squares or rectangles. Makes about 20 brownies.

COCONUT SQUARES

1 cup sifted all-purpose flour
¼ cup firmly packed brown sugar
⅓ cup softened butter or margarine
2 eggs
1 cup firmly packed brown sugar

¼ cup sifted all-purpose flour
½ teaspoon Calumet baking powder
1⅓ cups (about) Baker's Angel Flake coconut
1 teaspoon vanilla
1 cup chopped walnuts

Combine 1 cup flour and ¼ cup brown sugar. Add butter and blend well. Press firmly into an ungreased 9-inch square pan. Bake at 350° for 15 minutes.

Meanwhile, beat eggs until thick and light in color. Add 1 cup brown sugar gradually, beating until mixture is light and fluffy. Sift ¼ cup flour with the baking powder; fold into egg mixture. Mix in coconut, vanilla and nuts. Spread over baked crust in pan, and bake 20 to 25 minutes longer, or until lightly browned. Cool; cut in squares. Makes about 2 dozen.

DATE-NUT BARS

1¼ cups sifted cake flour, or
    1 cup sifted all-purpose
    flour
1 teaspoon Calumet
    baking powder
½ teaspoon salt
1 cup sugar
2 eggs, well beaten

¼ cup melted butter or
    margarine
1 tablespoon hot water
2 teaspoons grated orange
    rind (optional)
2 cups finely cut dates
1 cup chopped nuts

Sift flour with baking powder and salt. Gradually beat sugar into eggs. Stir in butter, water and orange rind. Add dates and nuts. Gradually add flour mixture, beating well. Spread batter evenly in a greased 13 × 9-inch pan. Bake at 325° for 25 to 30 minutes. Cool; cut in bars and roll in confectioners sugar, if desired. Makes 4 dozen.

COCONUT COOKIE BARS

½ cup butter or margarine
1½ cups graham cracker
    crumbs
2 cups Baker's Angel Flake
    coconut
1 cup chopped nuts
1½ cups miniature
    marshmallows
    (optional)

1 can (14 oz.) sweetened
    condensed milk
3 squares Baker's
    semi-sweet chocolate,
    melted

Preheat oven to 350°. Place butter in a 13 × 9-inch pan and place in oven to melt butter. Remove pan from oven, and sprinkle crumbs over butter, pressing down with a fork. Sprinkle coconut over crumbs; add a layer of nuts and marshmallows. Drizzle condensed milk evenly over the top. Bake at 350° for 25 to 30 minutes, or until golden brown. Remove from oven and drizzle with melted chocolate. Cool before cutting. Makes 48 small or 24 large bars.

Opposite: Coconut Cookie Bars

CRUNCHY COFFEE KUCHEN

1 cup all-purpose flour
1 cup firmly packed brown
    sugar
1½ teaspoons Calumet
    baking powder
½ teaspoon ground
    cinnamon
¼ teaspoon salt

½ cup vegetable shortening
1½ cups Post raisin bran or
    Post 40% bran flakes
1 teaspoon Maxwell House
    instant coffee
⅔ cup milk
1 egg, slightly beaten
¼ cup chopped pecans

Combine flour, brown sugar, baking powder, cinnamon and salt in a bowl. Cut in shortening until mixture is crumbly. Add cereal. Measure ⅓ cup of the mixture; set aside. Add instant coffee to remaining flour mixture. Stir in milk and egg; blend thoroughly. Pour into greased and floured 8- or 9-inch pie pan, or 8- or 9-inch square pan. Sprinkle with reserved mixture; then sprinkle with pecans. Bake at 350° for 30 to 35 minutes, or until cake tester inserted in center comes out clean. Cut in squares and serve warm.

FRUIT-FILLED COFFEE RING

2 cups cake flour, or 1¾
    cups all-purpose flour
2 teaspoons Calumet
    baking powder
1 teaspoon salt
¼ cup shortening
1 egg, slightly beaten
½ cup heavy cream

Pineapple or Lemon
    Filling
¾ cup Baker's Angel Flake
    coconut
¾ cup sifted confectioners
    sugar
1½ tablespoons lemon juice

Sift flour with baking powder and salt. Cut in shortening. Combine egg and cream; add to flour mixture and stir to form a soft dough. Turn out on a lightly floured board and pat or roll into a 12 × 7-inch rectangle. Spread filling evenly on dough; sprinkle with ½ cup of the coconut. Roll as for jelly roll, wetting edges to seal; cut into 1-inch slices. Arrange slices in a circle, cut sides down, on a greased baking sheet. Press together lightly to form a ring. Bake at 425° for 25 to 30 minutes, or until lightly browned. Remove from pan. Combine confectioners sugar and lemon juice and spread over rolls while still warm. Sprinkle with remaining coconut. Makes 12 rolls.

PINEAPPLE FILLING

1 can (8¼ oz.) crushed pineapple in syrup
1 tablespoon cornstarch
1 tablespoon sugar
Dash of salt
1 egg, slightly beaten
2 teaspoons lemon juice

Drain pineapple, reserving ⅓ cup syrup. Combine cornstarch, sugar and salt in saucepan. Blend in the measured syrup, the pineapple and egg; mix well. Cook and stir over medium heat until mixture is clear and thickened. Remove from heat and add lemon juice. Chill. Makes about 1 cup.

LEMON FILLING

½ cup sugar
2 tablespoons cornstarch
Dash of salt
6 tablespoons water
3 tablespoons lemon juice
1 egg yolk
1 teaspoon butter or margarine
½ teaspoon grated lemon rind

Combine sugar, cornstarch and salt in a saucepan. Stir in water and lemon juice. Cook and stir over medium heat until mixture comes to a boil and is smooth and shiny. Stir a small amount of the hot mixture into the egg yolk, mixing well. Return to remaining hot mixture. Continue cooking until mixture comes to a boil. Boil 1 minute, stirring constantly. Remove from heat; stir in butter and lemon rind. Makes ¾ cup.

GINGERBREAD

Cora says: "Some folks like this with whipped cream, hot applesauce or vanilla ice cream instead of the Lemon Sauce. Take your choice—they're all good."

1¼ cups sifted all-purpose flour
¾ teaspoon Calumet baking powder
½ teaspoon salt
¼ teaspoon baking soda
½ teaspoon ground cinnamon
½ teaspoon ground ginger
¼ teaspoon ground cloves
½ cup molasses
½ cup water
¼ cup shortening
¼ cup sugar
1 egg
Lemon Sauce

Sift flour with baking powder, salt, soda and spices. Combine molasses and water. Cream shortening. Gradually blend in sugar. Add egg and beat well. Add flour mixture, alternately with molasses mixture, a small amount at a time, beating after each addition until smooth. Pour batter into greased 8-inch square pan. Bake at 350° for 35 minutes, or until cake tester inserted into center comes out clean. Cut in squares. Serve warm or cooled with Lemon Sauce.

LEMON SAUCE

⅔ cup sugar
1 tablespoon cornstarch
⅛ teaspoon salt
1 cup water
1 tablespoon butter or margarine
1 teaspoon grated lemon rind
2 tablespoons lemon juice
2 drops yellow food coloring (optional)

Combine sugar, cornstarch and salt in saucepan; mix well. Gradually stir in water. Cook and stir over medium heat until mixture comes to a boil. Boil 3 minutes, stirring constantly. Remove from heat and add butter, lemon rind, lemon juice and coloring. Serve warm or chilled. Makes about 1⅓ cups.

Opposite: Gingerbread with Lemon Sauce

Sweet Breads that Satisfy

Don't be misled by the term "sweet breads." I just use the phrase to distinguish them from regular sandwich breads. The thing I like best about these is that they're not too sweet, so they're not appetite-spoilers before dinner. Great as after-school snacks.

QUICK SALLY LUNN

2 cups sifted cake flour	¾ cup milk
3 teaspoons Calumet baking powder	½ cup firmly packed brown sugar
½ teaspoon salt	1 teaspoon ground cinnamon
¼ cup shortening	
⅓ cup granulated sugar	1 tablespoon melted butter or margarine
2 eggs	

Sift flour with baking powder and salt. Cream shortening; add sugar and beat thoroughly. Add eggs, one at a time; beat well. Add flour mixture alternately with milk, beating well after each addition. Pour into a greased 9-inch square pan or 12 muffin pans. Mix together brown sugar, cinnamon and butter; sprinkle over batter. Bake at 400° for 20 to 25 minutes, or until cake tester inserted in center comes out clean. Cool 10 minutes. Remove from pan. Serve warm.

MOLASSES CEREAL BREAD

Cora says: "Try this tasty bread sliced and toasted and spread with softened cream cheese—or make a dessert 'sandwich' with your favorite jelly spread between two slices."

1½ cups Post 40% bran flakes	¾ teaspoon salt
1 cup milk	¼ teaspoon baking soda
2 cups sifted all-purpose flour	1 egg, beaten
	¼ cup molasses
⅔ cup sugar	¼ cup shortening, melted and cooled
2 teaspoons Calumet baking powder	

Soften cereal in milk. Sift flour with sugar, baking powder, salt and baking soda. Stir egg, molasses and melted shortening into softened cereal. Add flour mixture and stir just to moisten all flour. Pour into a greased 9 × 5-inch loaf pan. Bake at 325° for about 1 hour, or until cake tester inserted in center comes out clean. Cool in pan 10 minutes; remove from pan and finish cooling on rack.

Note: For easier slicing and mellowing of flavors, store bread overnight wrapped in wax paper, plastic wrap or aluminum foil.

ORANGE-COCONUT BREAD

Cora says: "Spread warm toasted slices of this delicious bread with a little butter or margarine, then top with orange marmalade. Instant pickup for a weary afternoon!"

3 cups sifted all-purpose
    flour
1 cup sugar
3 teaspoons Calumet
    baking powder
1 teaspoon salt
1⅓ cups (about) Baker's
    Angel Flake coconut,
    toasted

1 tablespoon grated
    orange rind
1 egg, well beaten
1½ cups milk
1 teaspoon vanilla

Sift flour with sugar, baking powder and salt; stir in coconut and orange rind. Combine egg, milk and vanilla; stir into flour mixture. (Do not beat.) Pour into greased 9 × 5-inch loaf pan. Bake at 350° for 1 hour and 10 minutes, or until cake tester inserted in center comes out clean. Cool in pan 10 minutes; remove from pan and finish cooling on rack. Cut into thin slices; toast, if desired.

Note: See Note under Molasses Cereal Bread.

Toasted Coconut: To toast coconut, thinly spread coconut in shallow baking pan. Toast at 350° for 7 to 12 minutes, or until lightly browned. Stir coconut or shake pan often to toast evenly.

BRAN PRUNE BREAD

1 cup chopped dried
    prunes
Boiling water
1¾ cups all-purpose flour
½ cup sugar
2½ teaspoons Calumet
    baking powder
1 teaspoon salt

1 egg, well beaten
1 cup milk
¼ cup molasses
¼ cup shortening, melted
1 cup Post 40% bran flakes
    or Post Grape-Nuts
    flakes
¼ cup chopped nuts

Cover prunes with boiling water. Let stand 2 minutes; drain. Mix flour with sugar, baking powder and salt. Combine egg, milk and molasses. Add to flour mixture. Add shortening and mix only enough to dampen flour. Fold in prunes, cereal and nuts. Pour into a greased 9 × 5-inch loaf pan. Bake at 350° for 55 to 60 minutes, or until done. Cool.

Note: See Note under Molasses Cereal Bread. Bread may also be baked in 3 individual (5½ × 3¼-inch) loaf pans; bake 35 to 40 minutes.

CRANBERRY-ORANGE NUT BREAD

2¼ cups all-purpose flour
¾ cup plus 2 tablespoons
    sugar
2 teaspoons Calumet
    baking powder
¾ teaspoon salt
½ teaspoon baking soda
1 cup coarsely chopped
    cranberries

½ cup chopped nuts
1 egg, well beaten
½ cup milk
½ cup orange juice
2 tablespoons shortening,
    melted

Mix flour with sugar, baking powder, salt and soda. Add cranberries and nuts. Combine egg, milk and orange juice. Add to flour mixture with melted shortening; mix until all flour is dampened. Pour into greased 9 × 5-inch loaf pan. Bake at 350° for 1 hour, or until cake tester inserted in center comes out clean. Cool in pan 10 minutes; then remove from pan and finish cooling on rack.

Note: See Note under Molasses Cereal Bread.

Opposite: Bran Prune Bread (front), Date-Nut Bread (left; recipe, p. 50), and Cranberry-Orange Nut Bread (right)

FAVORITE NUT BREAD

Cora says: "Tuck a few slices of this into the lunch boxes some day instead of the usual cookies."

3 cups sifted all-purpose flour	1 egg, well beaten
3 teaspoons Calumet baking powder	1⅓ cups milk
1½ teaspoons salt	¼ cup shortening, melted
1 cup firmly packed light brown sugar	1 cup finely chopped nuts

Sift flour with baking powder and salt; mix in brown sugar. Combine egg and milk. Add to flour mixture with shortening; mix just enough to dampen dry ingredients. Stir in nuts. Pour into a 9 × 5-inch loaf pan that has been lined on bottom with paper. Bake at 350° for 1 hour and 5 minutes, or until cake tester inserted in center comes out clean. Cool in pan 10 minutes; remove from pan and finish cooling on rack.

Note: See Note under Molasses Cereal Bread.

Date-Nut Bread *(Illustrated page 49).* Prepare Favorite Nut Bread as directed, reducing nuts to ½ cup and folding in 1 cup finely cut dates with nuts. Bake in 2 well-greased 4-cup ring molds or one 6-cup mold for 1 hour, if desired.

EVENING MAIN EVENTS

Country cooking—that's the heart of my cookbook, just like main dishes are probably the heart of your cooking. "What's for dinner?" is a question that must be heard in your home every day. Your brood is hungry again, and the truth of the matter is, so are you! Most families look forward to dinner most of all. They can relax then, get together and spend time chatting about the day's doings. I'm real proud of this collection of recipes; I've picked out the best of the lot I've tried over the years. Many of them have grass roots flavor—they're down-to-earth basics that have proven themselves favorites with one and all. You'll find out-of-the-ordinary ideas in this chapter, too. All of these recipes have one thing in common, though. None of them takes a lot of fussing over. I don't like to fuss, and I figure you probably don't, either. I know you don't always have lots of time to spend on making dinner, so I've included some quick-to-fix recipes. Even those that cook for a long time don't need watching, and the preparation is simple and easy. Remember, too, that some of the work on most all of the recipes can be done ahead of time.

There may be a few recipes here that you've thought of making before, but hesitated to attempt because you thought they'd be too difficult. Try my versions—bet you'll end up making them again and again. Easy, quick and best of all—delicious!

GLAZED CORNED BEEF BRISKET WITH CABBAGE

3 pounds corned beef
    brisket
½ cup chopped onion
2 garlic cloves, minced
2 bay leaves
1 medium head cabbage,
    cored and cut in
    wedges

1 cup Log Cabin syrup
½ cup prepared mustard
1 tablespoon prepared
    horseradish

Place brisket in heavy saucepan; add water to just cover, the onion, garlic and bay leaves. Cover, bring to a boil and simmer 1 hour. Drain, cover with fresh water and simmer until meat is tender, about 2 or 3 hours.

Remove brisket from pan, reserving liquid. Cook cabbage in reserved liquid until tender. Meanwhile, combine syrup, mustard and horseradish. Place brisket in shallow baking pan; spoon half the syrup mixture over meat and bake at 350° (basting frequently with remaining syrup mixture) about 20 minutes, or until well glazed. Heat pan drippings; pour over brisket. Serve with the cabbage and boiled potatoes and carrots, if desired. Makes 6 servings.

Opposite: Glazed Corned Beef Brisket with Cabbage

SAVORY BEEF POT ROAST

Cora says: "Good gravy! Serve with mashed potatoes to soak up that fine flavor."

4 pounds boneless beef chuck, round or rump roast	3 large onions, sliced
	1 teaspoon salt
	2 tablespoons all-purpose flour
1 tablespoon shortening	
½ cup water	½ cup cold water
¼ cup catsup (optional)	

Brown meat in shortening in a large heavy skillet or Dutch oven. Add ½ cup water, the catsup, onions and salt; cover tightly. Simmer 2 to 2½ hours, or until meat is tender. Add a little more water during cooking, if necessary. Place meat and onions on heated platter. Skim excess fat from liquid. Blend flour into ½ cup cold water; add to liquid. Cook and stir until gravy thickens. Serve over sliced pot roast. Makes 6 to 8 servings.

BEEF GOULASH

Cora says: "What could be better on a frosty winter night? Sprinkle caraway seed lightly over the noodles for an extra-savory taste."

6 medium onions, thinly sliced	1¾ cups beef broth*
	¼ cup tomato paste
1 clove garlic, minced	1½ teaspoons salt
¼ cup butter or margarine	1 teaspoon sugar
3 tablespoons paprika	½ teaspoon caraway seed
2 tablespoons vinegar	⅛ teaspoon pepper
2 pounds beef for stew, cut in 1½-inch cubes	

*or 2 beef bouillon cubes dissolved in 1¾ cups boiling water

Sauté onions and garlic in butter in a large skillet until golden brown. Stir in paprika and vinegar. Add beef cubes and brown lightly. Add remaining ingredients. Cover and simmer about 1

hour, or until beef is tender. Serve over hot cooked noodles,
if desired. Makes 4 cups or 6 to 8 servings.

BEEF RAGOUT

Cora says: "Here's a hearty, satisfying dinner—and there's nothing to do but combine the ingredients."

2 pounds beef for stew	1 can (16 oz.) tomatoes
2 celery stalks, cut in ½-inch pieces	⅓ cup Minute tapioca
	1 tablespoon sugar
1 medium onion, cut in 8 pieces	2½ teaspoons salt
	½ teaspoon pepper
2 medium carrots, halved and cut in 1-inch pieces	1 bay leaf

Combine all ingredients in Dutch oven or 2-quart casserole. Cover and bake at 300° for 3 hours. (No stirring is necessary.) Remove bay leaf. Makes about 7 cups or 7 servings.

SWISS STEAK

4 pounds beef round, ½ inch thick	¼ teaspoon pepper
	2 cups water
¾ cup all-purpose flour	2 cans (16 oz. each) tomatoes
4 to 6 tablespoons shortening	
	1 cup chopped celery
1 tablespoon salt	1 cup chopped green pepper
½ teaspoon savory	

Cut beef into 8 pieces. Coat with ½ cup of the flour and brown well in shortening in a large skillet. Place meat in a large shallow baking pan. Blend remaining flour and the seasonings into pan drippings. Gradually stir in water; then add tomatoes, celery and green pepper. Cook and stir until slightly thickened. Pour over meat; cover and bake at 325° for about 2 hours, or until meat is tender. Makes 8 servings.

CORNED BEEF HASH

3 cups chopped boiled
potatoes
2 cups chopped cooked
corned beef
½ cup finely chopped onion

½ cup (about) milk
½ teaspoon salt
Dash of pepper
3 to 4 tablespoons butter
or margarine

Combine potatoes, corned beef and onion; add enough milk to moisten and the salt and pepper. Melt butter in a skillet. Spread beef mixture evenly in pan and cook over low heat about 30 minutes, or until well browned on bottom. Fold over as for an omelet, if desired. Makes 4 servings.

CREAMED CHIPPED BEEF

1 jar (5 oz.) sliced dried
beef
¼ cup butter or margarine
¼ cup all-purpose flour

½ teaspoon salt
Dash of pepper
2 cups milk

Separate beef slices and shred. Cover with boiling water; drain well. Sauté beef in butter in skillet or saucepan until lightly browned. Blend in flour, salt and pepper. Slowly stir in milk. Cook and stir over medium heat until mixture thickens. Makes 2½ cups or 3 or 4 servings.

WIENER SCHNITZEL

8 thinly sliced veal cutlets
(about 1½ pounds)
Seasoned all-purpose
flour
2 eggs, slightly beaten
1½ cups (about) dry bread
crumbs

6 tablespoons butter or
margarine
Lemon slices
Chopped parsley or
watercress

Coat veal cutlets with seasoned flour. Dip in egg, then in bread crumbs to coat evenly. Sauté cutlets in butter in large skillet, about 10 minutes, turning to brown both sides. Garnish with lemon slices and chopped parsley or watercress. Serve with pan-browned potatoes, if desired. Makes 8 servings.

Opposite: Wiener Schnitzel

HAM AND SWEET POTATO SKILLET

Cora says: "Ham and sweet potatoes are natural go-togethers. The apples add a just-right flavor."

Whole cloves
1½ -pound (about) ham slice
2 tablespoons butter or
    margarine
¼ teaspoon dry mustard

1 cup Log Cabin syrup
2 cans (17 oz. each) sweet
    potatoes, drained*
1 cup drained canned
    pie-sliced apples

or cook 4 to 6 medium sweet potatoes; peel and slice while still warm

Insert cloves into one side of ham slice. Melt butter in a large heavy skillet. Blend in mustard and syrup. Cook and stir 5 minutes over medium heat. Add potatoes and cook 5 minutes, turning occasionally. Add apples and move potatoes and apples to sides of pan. Add ham slice, cloves side down, and cook 5 minutes on each side, basting apples and potatoes frequently with drippings. Makes 4 servings.

UPSIDE-DOWN HAM LOAF

1 pound ground cooked
    ham
1 pound ground raw pork
2 eggs, slightly beaten
1 cup cracker crumbs
1 cup milk
¼ teaspoon salt
⅛ teaspoon pepper

1 can (8 oz.) pineapple
    chunks, drained
Maraschino cherries,
    drained
¾ cup firmly packed brown
    sugar
¼ cup vinegar
2 teaspoons dry mustard

Combine ham, pork, eggs, cracker crumbs, milk, salt and pepper, mixing thoroughly.

Arrange pineapple and cherries in bottom of a 9 × 5-inch loaf pan. Combine sugar, vinegar and mustard; spread half the sugar mixture over the fruit. Top with meat mixture, packing firmly. Spread remaining sugar mixture over meat. Bake at 375° for 1½ hours. *Always cook pork thoroughly.* Let stand 10 minutes; then turn out of pan onto platter. Makes 8 servings.

SPARERIB-SAUERKRAUT BAKE

4 pounds spareribs
1½ teaspoons salt
½ teaspoon pepper
2 cans (28 oz. each) sauerkraut

2 cups diced tart apples
¾ cup diced onions
1½ teaspoons caraway seed
½ teaspoon pepper

Cut spareribs into 2- or 3-rib pieces. Place in shallow baking pan and sprinkle with salt and pepper. Bake at 450° for 30 minutes, turning occasionally, until browned. Reduce heat to 350° and bake 1 hour longer. Remove from oven; drain off fat. Combine sauerkraut with liquid, apples, onions, caraway seed and pepper, and spoon over ribs. Cover pan and continue baking at 350° about 1 hour longer, or until ribs are tender, adding a small amount of water if necessary. *Always cook pork thoroughly.* Makes 6 servings.

Note: Recipe may be doubled, using 9 pounds spareribs.

SWEET AND SOUR PORK CHOPS

Cora says: "Here's a sweet and sour combination borrowed from Chinese cooking—serve over hot cooked rice to enjoy every bit of the flavor."

6 pork chops
¼ cup all-purpose flour
1½ teaspoons salt
½ teaspoon pepper
½ teaspoon ground ginger
2 tablespoons oil
½ cup chopped onion

1 garlic clove, minced
¾ cup water
⅓ cup chili sauce
3 tablespoons vinegar
1½ tablespoons brown sugar
2 teaspoons soy sauce

Trim excess fat from pork chops. Combine flour, salt, pepper and ginger. Coat chops with seasoned flour and brown well in oil in large skillet. Move chops to sides of pan; add onion and garlic and sauté until onion is tender but not browned. Combine water, chili sauce, vinegar, brown sugar and soy sauce. Pour over chops; cover and simmer gently about 45 minutes, or until tender. *Always cook pork thoroughly.* Place chops on serving platter; skim excess fat from sauce and serve with chops. Makes 4 to 6 servings.

ORANGE-GLAZED ROAST PORK

Cora says: "Just three ingredients—but they add up to mighty good eating."

3-pound pork roast
½ cup orange juice

¼ cup firmly packed brown sugar

Place pork on rack in shallow roasting pan, and roast at 350° for about 2½ hours, or to an internal temperature of 185°. *Always cook pork thoroughly.* Meanwhile, combine orange juice and brown sugar; baste pork during last 30 minutes of roasting. Makes 6 servings.

APPLE AND SAUSAGE SUPPER

Cora says: "Sausages are usually a breakfast favorite. Surprise your family with this sausage supper come nippy weather. Maybe my Peach Cobbler (page 99) for dessert?"

1 medium cooking apple, cut into 8 wedges
2 tablespoons butter or margarine
1 medium green pepper, cut into thin strips
2 tablespoons diced scallions
8 link sausages, cut in chunks (about 1 lb.)

3 tablespoons brown sugar
2 tablespoons cornstarch
½ teaspoon salt
Dash of pepper
1 cup water
½ cup apple juice
2 tablespoons soy sauce
1 tablespoon vinegar
Hot cooked rice

Sauté apple in 2 tablespoons butter in skillet until tender; remove from skillet. Sauté green pepper and scallions in butter remaining in skillet until tender; remove from skillet. Sauté sausages in skillet until browned; pour off drippings. Combine brown sugar, cornstarch, ½ teaspoon salt and the pepper. Add 1 cup water, the apple juice, soy sauce and vinegar; mix well and pour over sausages. Cook and stir over medium heat until sauce is thickened and clear. Cover and simmer 10 minutes. Add apple, green pepper and scallions, and heat thoroughly. Serve over rice. Makes 4 cups sausage mixture or 4 servings.

Opposite: Apple and Sausage Supper

TASTY MEAT LOAF

1 pound ground beef
1 can (15 oz.) tomato
    sauce
⅓ cup dry bread crumbs
2 tablespoons finely
    chopped onion
2 tablespoons finely
    chopped green pepper
1 egg
½ teaspoon chili powder
½ teaspoon salt
Dash of pepper

Combine ground beef, ¼ cup of the tomato sauce, bread crumbs, onion, green pepper, egg, chili powder, salt and pepper; mix well. Shape into a loaf in a lightly greased baking pan. Bake at 350° for 30 minutes. Pour ¼ cup of the tomato sauce over loaf, and bake 15 minutes longer. Heat remaining tomato sauce and serve over sliced meat loaf. Makes 5 servings.

SWEDISH MEATBALLS

Cora says: "These tasty meatballs are equally welcome as an appetizer—or serve them with rice or mashed potatoes —delicious with the creamy gravy."

1 cup fine bread crumbs
1 cup milk
¼ cup minced onion
1 pound ground beef
1 egg, slightly beaten
1½ teaspoons salt
½ teaspoon ground nutmeg
⅛ teaspoon pepper
2 tablespoons butter or
    margarine
2 teaspoons all-purpose
    flour
1 cup hot water
1 bouillon cube
½ cup milk
½ cup light cream

Soak bread crumbs in 1 cup milk. Add onion, meat, egg and seasonings; mix thoroughly. Shape into 1-inch balls and sauté in butter in skillet until lightly browned on all sides. Remove from pan.

Blend flour into butter remaining in skillet. Add water, bouillon cube, ½ cup milk and the cream. Cook and stir until smooth and slightly thickened. Add the meatballs; cover and simmer gently 15 minutes. Makes 6 servings.

HAMBURGER AND POTATO PIE

3 tablespoons chopped onion	1 teaspoon paprika
	Dash of pepper
1 tablespoon butter or shortening	3 cups seasoned mashed potatoes
1 pound ground beef	1 egg yolk
1 can (16 oz.) tomatoes	2 tablespoons melted butter or margarine
1½ teaspoons salt	

Sauté onion in butter; add beef and brown well. Stir in tomatoes and seasonings. Pour into a 2-quart casserole.

Combine potatoes, egg yolk and melted butter. Beat until light and fluffy. Spread over meat mixture in casserole. Bake at 400° for 30 minutes, or until browned. Makes 4 or 5 servings.

CASSEROLE STEW

Cora says: "This thick, hearty dish needs only hot biscuits to round it out."

½ cup Post Grape-Nuts brand cereal	1 cup thinly sliced carrots
½ cup water	3 cups thinly sliced potatoes
1 pound ground beef	1 can (16 oz.) stewed tomatoes
2 teaspoons salt	
½ teaspoon pepper	
2 medium onions, coarsely chopped	

Combine cereal and water and let stand about 1 minute. Mix in ground beef, 1 teaspoon of the salt and ¼ teaspoon of the pepper. Brown meat well in a skillet; place in a 2-quart casserole. Add a layer of onions and a layer of carrots; top with potatoes. Sprinkle with remaining salt and pepper. Add the tomatoes; cover and bake at 350° for 1 hour. Uncover and continue baking 30 minutes longer, or until vegetables are tender. Makes about 8 cups or 6 servings.

STUFFED PEPPERS

Cora says: "Cereal adds a delightful flavor and texture difference to this all-time favorite main dish."

4 large green peppers	1 can (16 oz.) stewed
Boiling salted water	tomatoes
½ pound ground beef	½ cup Post Grape-Nuts
1 tablespoon (about) chili	brand cereal
powder	½ cup grated cheddar
¾ teaspoon garlic salt	cheese
¼ teaspoon salt	

Cut thin slices from tops of green peppers; remove seeds. Parboil in boiling salted water for 5 to 8 minutes; drain. Brown meat well in a skillet; stir in chili powder, garlic salt and salt. Remove from heat; add ½ cup of the tomatoes and the cereal. Spoon meat mixture into green peppers, using about ½ cup for each. Place in a greased shallow baking dish. Pour remaining tomatoes over the peppers; sprinkle with cheese. Bake at 375° for 25 minutes. Makes 2 cups filling or 4 servings.

FLAVORFUL BRAISED LAMB

Cora says: "The seasonings make all the difference here— try them and see if they don't spark the lamb flavor."

¼ cup all-purpose flour	2 medium onions,
2 teaspoons salt	chopped
1 teaspoon celery seed	¼ cup oil
1 teaspoon caraway seed	2 cups water
1 teaspoon rosemary	1 teaspoon tarragon
leaves	vinegar
3 pounds lean lamb, cut	
into 1-inch cubes	

Combine flour and seasonings. Coat lamb cubes with seasoned flour, and brown meat and onions in hot oil in large saucepan. Stir in water and vinegar. Cover and simmer about 45 minutes, or until meat is tender. Makes about 6 cups or 6 servings.

LAMB STEW

Cora says: "Now here's a change! Lamb with cranberry sauce—and the ginger and oregano add even more zing."

2 pounds lamb shoulder, cut in 1-inch cubes	¾ cup finely chopped onions
2 tablespoons oil or shortening	1 garlic clove, minced
1½ cups water	1 teaspoon salt
1 cup Burgundy wine or unsweetened grapefruit juice	⅛ teaspoon pepper
	¾ cup whole berry cranberry sauce
1 can (6 oz.) tomato paste	¼ teaspoon ground ginger
	¼ teaspoon oregano

Brown lamb well in oil in skillet or large saucepan. Add water, wine, tomato paste, onions, garlic, salt and pepper. Cover and simmer 45 minutes. Add cranberry sauce, ginger and oregano, and simmer 45 minutes longer, or until lamb is tender. Serve with hot cooked rice, if desired. Makes 6 to 8 servings.

LIVER AND TOMATOES

Cora says: "You'll be surprised how different liver tastes cut into strips. Even stubborn liver-haters enjoy this well-seasoned dish."

2 bacon slices, halved	½ cup chopped onion
¼ cup all-purpose flour	½ cup diced celery
1 teaspoon salt	1 can (16 oz.) tomatoes
¼ teaspoon pepper	1 teaspoon salt
1 pound beef liver	½ teaspoon chili powder

Fry bacon in large skillet until crisp. Remove from skillet; set aside. Combine flour, 1 teaspoon salt and the pepper. Remove heavy membranes and veins from liver and cut into strips. Coat with seasoned flour; brown with onion and celery in bacon drippings in skillet. Add tomatoes, 1 teaspoon salt and the chili powder. Cook, stirring occasionally, 10 minutes, or until liver is tender. Garnish with bacon. Makes 4 to 5 servings.

Plain and Fancy Fowl

For real economy, you'll have to go a long way before you can beat chicken or turkey. And one of the nicest things about poultry is that it's so versatile. You can combine it successfully with darn near any other ingredients that suit you.

STEWED CHICKEN

Cora says: "Dinner's never very far from made when you start with the bonus of already-made chilled chicken and stock on hand."

2- to 3-pound chicken	Dash of thyme
3 cups water	1 medium onion, halved
1½ teaspoons salt	1 celery stalk with leaves
1 or 2 bay leaves	1 medium carrot, sliced
¼ teaspoon whole black pepper	

Place chicken in heavy saucepan; add water, salt, bay leaves, pepper, thyme and vegetables. Bring to a boil; cover and simmer about 1 hour, or until chicken is tender. Remove chicken from pan; strain stock. (If stock measures more than 2 cups, boil to reduce.) Remove and discard skin and bones from chicken. Skim off chicken fat. There should be 2 to 2½ cups (about ¾ lb.) cooked chicken, about ½ cup fat and about 2 cups stock.

Note: Chicken may be stewed in advance; chill chicken, stock and fat separately. Recipe may be doubled using a 4½- to 6-pound dressed stewing chicken.

Chicken Fricassee. Blend ¼ cup all-purpose flour into ¼ cup chicken fat (or use butter or margarine) in a saucepan. Cook and stir until mixture thickens and comes to a boil. Add 2 to 2½ cups diced cooked chicken, and heat thoroughly. Serve over hot cooked rice or noodles, and sprinkle with chopped parsley, if desired. Makes about 3½ cups or 4 or 5 servings.

Chicken à la King. Sauté 1½ cups (about ¼ pound) sliced
mushrooms, ¾ cup green pepper strips and 1 tablespoon
chopped onion in ½ cup chicken fat (or use butter or margarine) until tender and lightly browned. Blend in ½ cup all-purpose flour, 2 teaspoons salt and a dash of pepper. Gradually
stir in 2 cups chicken stock and 2 cups milk. Cook and stir until
mixture comes to a boil and is thickened. Stir in ½ cup light
cream or half and half, 2 to 2½ cups diced cooked chicken,
¼ cup diced pimiento and 1 tablespoon sherry wine (optional);
heat thoroughly. Serve over hot cooked rice or toast or biscuits,
if desired. Makes about 7 cups or 8 servings.

OLD-FASHIONED TURKEY PIE
(Illustrated page 68)

1 package (10 oz.) Birds Eye 5 minute peas and carrots	2 cups turkey or chicken stock
¼ cup butter or margarine	1 cup milk
5 tablespoons all-purpose flour	3 cups thin strips cooked turkey
½ teaspoon salt	12 cooked small white onions
¼ teaspoon poultry seasoning	1 cup cooked diced potatoes
Dash of pepper	Biscuit Topping

Prepare peas and carrots as directed on package; drain. Melt
butter in saucepan; blend in flour, salt, poultry seasoning and
pepper. Gradually add stock and milk. Cook and stir over medium heat until mixture thickens. Add peas and carrots, turkey,
onions and potatoes. Pour into a greased shallow baking dish.
Cut Biscuit Topping into squares or wedges and place over hot
turkey mixture. Bake at 425° for 20 to 25 minutes or until topping is golden brown. Makes about 8 cups turkey mixture or
6 servings.

Biscuit Topping. Mix 1⅓ cups all-purpose flour with 1½
teaspoons Calumet baking powder and ½ teaspoon salt. Cut
in 5 tablespoons shortening. Gradually add ½ cup (about)
milk, stirring with a fork to form a soft dough. Knead for 30 seconds on a lightly floured board. Roll in shape of baking dish,
but about 1½ inches smaller.

CHICKEN CACCIATORE

¼ cup olive oil
3 pounds frying chicken
   pieces
2 medium onions, sliced
2 cloves garlic, crushed
1 can (16 oz.) tomatoes

1 can (8 oz.) tomato sauce
1 teaspoon salt
1 teaspoon leaf basil
½ teaspoon celery seed
¼ teaspoon pepper
2 bay leaves

Heat oil in large skillet. Add chicken and brown slowly on all sides. Remove chicken from skillet. Add onions and garlic to oil remaining in skillet; sauté until tender but not browned. Stir in tomatoes, tomato sauce and seasonings. Add chicken, baste with sauce; cover and simmer 30 minutes. Uncover and simmer 20 minutes longer, turning chicken occasionally. Remove bay leaves and skim off excess fat. Arrange chicken on warm platter; top with sauce. Makes 6 servings.

BARBECUE GLAZED ROAST CHICKEN

Cora says: "Here's my variation of a traditional Chinese taste."

¼ cup butter or margarine
½ cup Log Cabin syrup
¼ cup lemon juice
¼ cup soy sauce
1 teaspoon garlic salt

1 teaspoon ground ginger
5-pound (about) roasting
   chicken
½ cup chopped scallions

Melt butter in small saucepan. Blend in syrup, lemon juice, soy sauce, garlic salt and ginger. Brush inside cavity of chicken with some of the sauce. Place scallions in chicken cavity. Truss chicken, and place breast side up on rack in shallow roasting pan; brush with sauce. Roast at 325° about 3½ hours, basting at 30-minute intervals with remaining sauce. (If drippings begin to char during roasting, add small amount of water.) Place chicken on serving platter. Pour pan drippings into saucepan and simmer until mixture is slightly thickened. Serve with chicken. Makes about 5 to 6 servings.

Opposite: Old-Fashioned Turkey Pie (recipe, p. 67)

SWISS CHICKEN AND SAUCE

2 tablespoons all-purpose
  flour
½ teaspoon salt
  Dash of white pepper
2½ to 3 pounds frying
  chicken pieces
¼ cup oil

¾ cup water
2 chicken bouillon cubes
1 egg, beaten
3 tablespoons lemon juice
2 tablespoons chopped
  parsley

Combine flour, salt and pepper. Dredge chicken pieces with flour mixture and brown lightly on all sides in oil in skillet. Add water and bouillon cubes; cover and simmer about 30 minutes, or until chicken is tender. Remove chicken from pan. Combine egg and lemon juice and blend into stock in skillet. Add parsley and heat gently. (Do not boil.) Serve over chicken. Makes 4 or 5 servings.

CHICKEN-BROCCOLI BAKE

1 package (10 oz.) Birds
  Eye 5 minute chopped
  broccoli
1 package (4 oz.) medium
  noodles
2 cups chopped cooked
  chicken
1 cup (½ pt.) sour cream
1 can (10¾ oz.) condensed
  cream of chicken soup
¼ cup diced pitted ripe
  olives

2 tablespoons chopped
  pimiento
1 tablespoon instant
  minced onion
1 teaspoon salt
½ teaspon Worcestershire
  sauce
1 tablespoon butter or
  margarine, melted
½ cup soft bread crumbs
1 cup grated Swiss cheese

Prepare broccoli as directed on package; drain. Cook noodles as directed on package; drain.

Combine chicken, sour cream, soup, olives, pimiento, onion, salt and Worcestershire sauce. Add butter to bread crumbs and mix well. Place noodles in a greased shallow 2-quart baking dish. Sprinkle with one third of the cheese. Add broccoli; sprinkle with half of the remaining cheese. Pour on the chicken mixture. Sprinkle with the remaining cheese and then with bread crumbs. Bake at 350° for 1 hour, or until golden brown. Makes 4 or 5 servings.

CHICKEN AND BROCCOLI CASSEROLE

Cora says: "Add a tossed salad, piping hot rolls, and your dinner's a hit!"

1 package (10 oz.) Birds Eye 5 minute chopped broccoli
4 ounces spaghetti
⅓ cup butter or margarine
⅓ cup all-purpose flour
2 teaspoons salt
⅛ teaspoon pepper
2 cups milk*

1 cup chicken stock*
1 tablespoon finely chopped onion
1½ cups diced cooked chicken
1 tablespoon lemon juice
⅔ cup grated cheddar cheese

*or 3 cups milk and omit chicken stock

Prepare broccoli as directed on package; drain. Cook spaghetti as directed on package; drain.

Melt butter in saucepan; blend in flour, salt and pepper. Gradually stir in milk and chicken stock. Add onion. Cook and stir over medium heat until sauce is thickened. Add broccoli, spaghetti, chicken and lemon juice. Mix well and pour into a 1½-quart baking dish; sprinkle with cheese. Bake at 350° for 30 minutes. Then place under the broiler until cheese is lightly browned. Makes 6 cups or 6 servings.

SAUTEED CHICKEN LIVERS

2 slices bacon, diced
1 medium onion, cut in eighths
⅓ cup all-purpose flour
1 teaspoon salt
⅛ teaspoon pepper

1 pound chicken livers, cut in half
½ cup sliced celery
⅔ cup water
½ teaspoon salt

Fry bacon in skillet until almost crisp. Add onion and sauté until onion is tender and bacon is crisp, about 2 minutes. Combine flour, 1 teaspoon salt and the pepper; dredge chicken livers in flour mixture, and sauté in skillet until browned, about 5 minutes. Add celery, water and ½ teaspoon salt. Bring to a boil, stirring frequently. Serve with hot cooked rice, if desired. Makes 2⅔ cups chicken liver mixture or 4 servings.

TURKEY OR CHICKEN CROQUETTES

Cora says: "This is a fine way to use up leftover turkey or chicken. Make the croquettes special by serving with my Carrot Marmalade (page 20)."

3 tablespoons butter or margarine
⅓ cup all-purpose flour
½ teaspoon salt
½ teaspoon ground thyme
⅛ teaspoon pepper
1 cup turkey or chicken broth
2 cups finely chopped cooked turkey or chicken

1 teaspoon chopped parsley
1 egg, slightly beaten
1 egg
2 tablespoons milk
1½ cups soft bread crumbs
Shortening

Melt butter in saucepan over low heat. Blend in flour, salt, thyme and pepper; stir in broth. Cook and stir over low heat until slightly thickened. Add turkey and parsley. Remove from heat. Stir a small amount of the hot mixture into the beaten egg, mixing well. Return to remaining hot mixture, and continue cooking about 1 minute. Cool; then shape into 12 croquettes.

Combine egg and milk; beat well. Roll croquettes in the crumbs; then dip in egg mixture. Roll again in crumbs and let stand for about 1 hour. Fry croquettes in about 1 inch hot (375°) shortening for about 2 minutes on each side. Drain on absorbent paper. Serve with tart red jelly, if desired. Makes 6 servings.

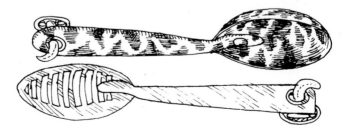

Surprise the family some night with something they've never had before—maybe one of my scrumptious fish or seafood dishes, my Fluffy Omelet or Corn Soufflé. Even those you thought were strictly meat-and-potato eaters will be happily enthusiastic!

SEAFOOD NEWBURG

¼ cup minced onion
1 tablespoon butter or margarine
1 tablespoon paprika
1 teaspoon salt
¼ teaspoon white pepper
Dash of cayenne
1 tablespoon water
1¼ cups light cream or half and half

¼ cup sherry wine
1 tablespoon lemon juice
4 cups hot thick White Sauce
4 cups cooked seafood and fish*
Hot buttered toast or cooked rice

*use at least 2 cups lobster, shrimp, scallops or crab meat, and add flaked drained tuna or flaked cooked cod, haddock, halibut, sole or other fish

Sauté onion in butter until tender but not browned. Blend paprika, salt, pepper and cayenne with water. Add cream, wine, lemon juice, the onion and the spice mixture to White Sauce in top of a double boiler. Heat over hot water, stirring frequently. Add seafood and fish and heat thoroughly. Keep warm over hot water. Serve on toast or rice. Makes about 8 cups or 8 to 10 servings.

White Sauce. Heat 6 tablespoons butter or margarine with 3 cups milk over boiling water until very hot. Blend ½ cup all-purpose flour with 1 cup milk until very smooth; add 1½ teaspoons salt. Stir flour mixture into hot milk mixture. Cook and stir until thickened. Makes 4 cups.

Note: The Newburg sauce (without seafood) may be prepared and frozen up to a month in advance. Thaw overnight in refrigerator and reheat over boiling water. If necessary, blend with a hand beater until smooth. Add seafood and fish, and heat.

FLAKED FISH CASSEROLE

Cora says: "Even families who don't like fish go for this dish. Beating the egg whites makes it lighter than most casseroles."

2 egg yolks	2 cans (7 oz. each) tuna or
2 cups milk	salmon, drained and
½ cup finely chopped	flaked, or 2 cups flaked
celery	cooked mild-flavored
2 tablespoons Minute	fish
tapioca	2 tablespoons chopped
1 tablespoon finely	parsley
chopped onion	2 egg whites, stiffly beaten
1½ teaspoons salt	½ cup soft buttered bread
Dash of pepper	crumbs

Mix egg yolks with a small amount of the milk in saucepan. Add remaining milk, the celery, tapioca, onion, salt and pepper; mix well and let stand 5 minutes. Bring to a boil over medium heat, stirring constantly. Remove from heat. Add tuna and parsley. Gradually fold into beaten egg whites. Spoon into greased 1½-quart casserole. Top with bread crumbs. Bake at 350° for about 50 minutes, or until firm and lightly browned. Makes about 4 cups or 4 to 6 servings.

CODFISH CAKES

Cora says: "Try this with my Coleslaw Cooler (page 30)— and Indian Pudding (page 101) for dessert—for a different and delicious meal."

1 cup shredded codfish	Dash of pepper
Boiling water	Dash of ground nutmeg
2½ cups diced raw potatoes	(optional)
1 egg, slightly beaten	
1 tablespoon butter or	
margarine	

Scald codfish with boiling water several times; drain well. Combine codfish and potatoes in a saucepan. Cover with boiling water and cook until potatoes are tender. Drain thoroughly and mash well. Add egg, butter and seasonings; beat until light and fluffy. Shape into patties and fry in well-greased skillet, turning to brown both sides. Makes 4 servings.

SCALLOPED OYSTERS

Cora says: "Cereal nuggets give surprise flavor to this tasty oyster dish."

½ cup chopped onion
¼ cup chopped celery
¼ cup butter or margarine
1 cup Post Grape-Nuts
   brand cereal
1 teaspoon salt
1½ pints fresh oysters
Milk

Sauté onion and celery in butter in saucepan; stir in cereal and salt. Spread half the cereal mixture in bottom of a shallow 8-inch square baking dish. Drain oysters, measuring liquid. Add milk to liquid to make ¾ cup. Arrange oysters in single layer in baking dish. Sprinkle with remaining cereal mixture and slowly pour in measured liquid. Bake at 400° for about 25 minutes, or until topping is lightly browned. Serve with lemon juice, if desired. Makes 4 or 5 servings.

SPICY SCALLOPS

Cora says: "Could've called these Deviled Scallops, but that didn't seem right—they just taste too heavenly."

¾ pound fresh scallops, or
   1 package (12 oz.)
   frozen scallops,
   thawed
¼ cup all-purpose flour
¼ cup butter or margarine
½ cup chili sauce
1 tablespoon chopped
   parsley
2 teaspoons lemon juice
½ teaspoon dry mustard
⅛ teaspoon salt
Dash of cayenne

Dry scallops with absorbent paper and coat lightly with flour. Sauté in butter in skillet for about 5 minutes, or until lightly browned, turning frequently. Combine remaining ingredients; pour over scallops and simmer 5 minutes. Serve over hot cooked rice, if desired. Makes 4 servings.

FLUFFY OMELET

Cora says: "Here's a spectacular-looking omelet that can serve as either main dish or dessert, depending on the filling you choose."

2 tablespoons Minute tapioca	1 tablespoon butter or margarine
¾ teaspoon salt	4 egg whites
⅛ teaspoon pepper	4 egg yolks
¾ cup milk	

Combine tapioca, salt and pepper in saucepan; add milk. Cook and stir over medium heat until mixture comes to a boil. Stir in butter. Remove from heat and cool slightly.

Meanwhile, beat egg whites until stiff. Beat egg yolks until thick and lemon colored. Gradually blend tapioca mixture into egg yolks; fold into egg whites. Pour into a hot buttered 10-inch skillet. Cook over low heat for 3 minutes. Then bake at 350° for 15 minutes, or until a knife inserted in center comes out clean. Cut across at right angle to handle of pan, being careful not to cut all the way through. Carefully fold from handle to opposite side, and turn out onto serving platter. Fill and top with Spanish Sauce (see page 78) or Creamed Chipped Beef (see page 56), if desired.

Apricot Omelet. Prepare Fluffy Omelet as directed, and spread with apricot jam before folding. Fold, place on serving platter and sprinkle with confectioners sugar.

Cheese Omelet. Prepare Fluffy Omelet as directed, adding ½ cup grated American cheese with the butter. Remove from heat and stir until cheese is melted.

Opposite: Fluffy Omelet with Spanish Sauce (recipe, p. 78)

SPANISH SAUCE *(Illustrated page 76)*

Cora says: "Here's a basic tomato sauce that's equally at home on meats or vegetables."

¼ cup chopped green pepper
¼ cup chopped onion
2 tablespoons butter or margarine
1 can (4 oz.) sliced mushrooms

1 can (16 oz.) tomatoes
2 teaspoons sugar
1 tablespoon Minute tapioca
½ teaspoon salt
Dash of cayenne

Sauté green pepper and onion in butter in large saucepan until onion is tender but not browned. Stir in remaining ingredients. Let stand 5 minutes. Cook and stir over low heat about 15 minutes, or until slightly thickened. Makes 2¼ cups.

SHRIMP CREOLE

Cora says: "Folks in Louisiana aren't the only ones who can enjoy this dish. If you clean and cook the shrimp in advance, there'll be nothing to your right-before-dinner preparation."

½ cup diced celery
¼ cup minced onion
¼ cup diced green pepper
3 tablespoons butter or margarine
1 tablespoon all-purpose flour
1 teaspoon salt
1 teaspoon sugar
Dash of pepper

1 can (16 oz.) tomatoes
1 bay leaf
1 sprig parsley
¾ pound (1½ cups) shrimp, cleaned and cooked, or 2 cans (5 or 7 oz. each) shrimp
¼ teaspoon Worcestershire sauce
Hot cooked rice

Sauté celery, onion and green pepper in butter in saucepan until tender but not browned. Blend in flour, salt, sugar and pepper. Stir in tomatoes; add bay leaf and parsley. Simmer 30 minutes. Remove bay leaf and parsley. Add shrimp and Worcestershire sauce and heat thoroughly. Serve over hot cooked rice. Makes 4 servings.

CORN SOUFFLE

Cora says: "Here's an easy soufflé that wins raves every time."

2 teaspoons finely chopped onion	1 teaspoon salt
	⅛ teaspoon pepper
1 package (10 oz.) Birds Eye 5 minute sweet whole kernel corn, thawed	1 cup milk
	1 tablespoon chopped parsley
	3 egg whites
2 tablespoons butter or margarine	3 egg yolks
3 tablespoons Minute tapioca	

Sauté onion and corn in butter in saucepan until onion is tender, about 5 minutes. Add tapioca, salt, pepper and milk; let stand 5 minutes. Cook and stir over medium heat until mixture comes to a full boil. Remove from heat and add parsley. Allow to cool slightly while beating eggs.

Beat egg whites until stiff. Beat egg yolks until thick and lemon colored. Gradually add tapioca mixture to egg yolks, blending well. Fold in egg whites. Spoon into 1½-quart baking dish. Place dish in pan of hot water and bake at 350° for 50 minutes, or until soufflé is firm. Serve plain or with mild-flavored cheese sauce, if desired. Makes 4 to 6 servings.

ROUNDING OUT THE MAIN MEAL

Dress up any meal with these winning combinations. These are the "extras" that really can perk up a meal, change it from a so-so supper to one that makes everyone sit up and take notice. If you're like me, you have at least one family member whose nose automatically wrinkles at any mention of the word vegetables. Convert a stubborn case like this with one of my recipes. These are so popular you'll find yourself with demands for second helpings! And don't think of these vegetables just for dinner time or your main meal. Some of the recipes would make a nice lunch, or a different snack or mini-meal. No reason in the world, for example, why you couldn't have my Corn Fritters for a delightful main course sometime. How about Zesty Zucchini Bake in the summer, when your green thumb has produced an abundance of fresh zucchini? Makes my mouth water just to think of it.

My recipes aren't fancy, but they have a different twist. Give them a try. We all know vegetables are good for you—but not much good to anybody if no one will eat them. I treat vegetables so that they keep the honest-to-goodness fresh taste they start out with.

NEW ENGLAND BAKED BEANS

Cora says: "Here's a delicious country-baked standby — serve with my Boston Brown Bread (page 34)."

4 cups dried pea or navy beans	1 teaspoon salt
Cold water	½ teaspoon pepper
1 whole onion	1 cup Log Cabin syrup
1 teaspoon salt	2 cups water
2 whole onions	½ pound salt pork, scored
4 whole cloves	¼ cup firmly packed brown
2 teaspoons dry mustard	sugar

Place beans in large saucepan; add enough water to cover by at least 2 inches. Let stand overnight. (*Or* bring to a boil, boil 2 minutes, remove from heat and let stand 1 hour.) Add 1 onion and 1 teaspoon salt; bring to a boil. Cover loosely, reduce heat and simmer very slowly for 1 hour. Drain, discarding liquid and the onion.

Stud each of 2 onions with 2 cloves. Place in 2½-quart bean pot or heavy casserole with tight-fitting lid. Combine mustard, 1 teaspoon salt and the pepper in large saucepan. Stir in syrup, 2 cups water and the beans. Bring to a boil; pour into bean pot and top with salt pork. Cover and bake at 250° for 4 hours. Remove from oven, sprinkle with brown sugar and continue baking, uncovered, 30 minutes longer. Makes 2 quarts or 8 to 16 servings.

GREEN BEANS AND CELERY

1 package (9 oz.) Birds Eye 5 minute cut or French-style green beans	¾ cup water ¾ teaspoon salt 1 tablespoon butter or margarine
1½ cups sliced celery	

Place beans, celery, water and salt in saucepan. Bring to a boil over medium-high heat, separating beans with a fork. Reduce heat; cover and simmer until beans and celery are just tender, about 5 minutes. Add more water during cooking if necessary to prevent sticking. Drain; add butter. Makes about 2½ cups or 4 or 5 servings.

BEETS IN ORANGE SAUCE

1 can (16 oz.) sliced beets	2 teaspoons grated orange rind
1 tablespoon cornstarch	¼ teaspoon salt
¼ cup orange juice	⅛ teaspoon garlic salt (optional)
1 tablespoon butter or margarine	

Drain beets, reserving ½ cup liquid. Blend cornstarch with beet liquid in a saucepan. Add orange juice, butter, orange rind, salt and garlic salt. Cook and stir over medium heat until mixture thickens and comes to a boil. Add beets, and heat thoroughly. Makes about 2 cups or 4 servings.

SWEET AND SOUR CABBAGE

⅓ cup chopped onion	½ cup water
½ cup butter or margarine	½ cup vinegar
1 head red cabbage, shredded (about 3 pounds)	¼ cup Log Cabin syrup 1 tablespoon salt ¼ teaspoon pepper

Sauté onion in butter in large heavy saucepan until tender. Add cabbage; cook and stir until softened. Add remaining ingredients. Bring to boil. Cover and simmer about 1¼ hours, or until very tender. Makes about 4½ cups or 8 servings.

PIQUANT CARROTS *(Illustrated page 84)*

2 cups sliced carrots, or 8 to 10 (about) small whole carrots
1 cup water
½ cup (about) orange juice
2 teaspoons cornstarch
1 tablespoon butter or margarine

1 teaspoon sugar
½ teaspoon grated orange rind
¼ teaspoon salt
2 dashes ground nutmeg

Cook carrots in saucepan with water until tender, about 10 minutes. Drain, reserving liquid. Add orange juice to liquid to make 1 cup. Blend cornstarch with measured liquid in saucepan. Add butter, sugar, orange rind, salt and nutmeg. Cook and stir over medium heat until mixture thickens and comes to a boil. Add carrots and heat thoroughly. Sprinkle with chopped parsley, if desired. Makes about 2 cups or 4 servings.

CORN FRITTERS

Cora says: "Try these for a satisfying lunch some day—or as a fine go-along with ham or pork."

1 package (10 oz.) Birds Eye 5 minute sweet whole kernel corn
½ cup all-purpose flour
¾ teaspoon Calumet baking powder
1 teaspoon salt

⅛ teaspoon pepper
3 tablespoons milk
2 tablespoons liquid shortening
2 eggs, well beaten
Fat for frying
Log Cabin syrup

Thaw corn, draining well. Mix flour with baking powder, salt and pepper. Add milk and shortening to eggs; add to dry ingredients, blending well. Stir in corn. Drop batter from tablespoon into about ½ inch of hot fat in a skillet. Fry fritters until golden brown on both sides, about 5 minutes. Drain on absorbent paper. Serve with syrup. Makes 10 to 12 fritters or 5 or 6 servings.

GLAZED ONIONS

16 small white onions,
    peeled*
Boiling salted water*
Whole cloves

¼ cup Log Cabin syrup
1 tablespoon butter or
    margarine

*or 2 jars (15½ oz. each) small white onions, drained; do not parboil

Cook onions in salted water about 15 minutes or until tender; drain. Insert a clove in each onion and place in a shallow baking pan. Pour syrup over onions; dot with butter. Bake at 350° for 30 minutes, basting onions frequently. Makes about 2 cups or 4 servings.

GLAZED TURNIPS

3 medium white turnips,
    diced (about 3 cups),
    or 1 medium rutabaga,
    diced (about 3½ cups)

Boiling salted water
3 tablespoons butter or
    margarine
⅓ cup Log Cabin syrup

Add turnips to boiling salted water to cover. Cook 15 to 20 minutes, or until tender; drain. Heat butter with syrup in a skillet. Add turnips and sauté until glazed, turning occasionally. Garnish with parsley, if desired. Makes 2½ cups or 5 or 6 servings.

ZESTY ZUCCHINI BAKE

3 medium onions, sliced
1 garlic clove, minced
⅓ cup oil
1 can (28 oz.) tomatoes
2 teaspoons salt
⅛ teaspoon pepper
2 teaspoons oregano

1 tablespoon wine vinegar
8 medium zucchini (about
    3 pounds), cut into
    ¼-inch slices
3 tablespoons grated
    Parmesan cheese

Sauté onions and garlic in oil in skillet or saucepan until lightly browned and tender. Add tomatoes, seasonings and vinegar. Bring to a boil and simmer 1 minute. Arrange zucchini slices in greased 3-quart casserole. Top with tomato–onion mixture; sprinkle with cheese. Bake at 400° for about 1 hour, or until zucchini is tender. Makes 10 cups or 8 to 10 servings.

Opposite: Glazed Turnips (front), Zesty Zucchini Bake (left), and Piquant Carrots (right; recipe, p. 83)

HASHED POTATO BAKE

2 tablespoons butter or
  margarine
1 teaspoon all-purpose
  flour
1¼ teaspoons salt
¼ teaspoon ground nutmeg

⅛ teaspoon pepper
1 cup heavy cream
4 cooked medium
  potatoes, diced
2 cups finely chopped
  onions

Melt butter in a saucepan; blend in flour and add salt, nutmeg and pepper. Gradually add cream; cook and stir over medium heat until slightly thickened. Add potatoes and onions, and pour into a greased 1-quart casserole. Bake at 350° for 30 minutes, or until potatoes are lightly browned. Makes about 3 cups or 6 servings.

BAKED ACORN SQUASH

3 medium acorn squash
⅓ to ½ cup Log Cabin
  syrup
3 tablespoons butter or
  margarine

Salt
Ground nutmeg

Cut squash in halves or quarters; remove seeds. Pour boiling water into a shallow baking dish to just cover the bottom. Place squash, cut side down, in dish. Bake at 400° about 30 minutes. Turn cut side up in pan; place 1 to 1½ tablespoons syrup and ½ tablespoon butter in each cavity. Sprinkle with salt and nutmeg. Continue baking 20 to 30 minutes longer, or until squash is tender, basting once or twice with syrup. Makes 6 servings.

DOWN-HOME DESSERTS
TO DAZZLE 'EM

There are a lot of people who think a meal isn't much without dessert—and I'm one of them. It's the high point of the meal. "Saving the best till last" is how I think of it, and I guess most people—grown-ups and kids—would agree. All of my recipes are special to me —hope they will be to you, too. What you prefer is, as they say, just a matter of taste. So—here's my prize collection of blue-ribbon treats, desserts to be proud of whether you enter them in contests or not. I know you're busy, but these pay big dividends. There's something about the smell of a fresh-baked cake that puts a smile on the most gloomy face and the sight of a frozen parfait that'll win praise from the hardest heart. You can make most of these ahead of time, when it suits you. Have them in reserve when friends come over for dessert and coffee. Although these recipes will all make guests happy, don't save them for special occasions only. I'm partial to family, and one of these dessert triumphs never fails to cause delight. So gladden everybody's day with homemade dessert. I guarantee—it'll say "I love you" every time.

Warm from the Oven

Mmm—what smells so good? Can't top the aroma of home-baked chocolate cake, apple pie, pudding, peach cobbler or whatever else you want to be complimented on. Make your folks happy by whipping up a special treat—just because it's today!

WELLESLEY FUDGE CAKE

4 squares Baker's unsweetened chocolate	1 teaspoon salt
	½ cup shortening*
	1¼ cups sugar
½ cup hot water	3 eggs
½ cup sugar	Milk*
2 cups sifted cake flour	1 teaspoon vanilla
1 teaspoon baking soda	

*with butter, use ¾ cup milk; with vegetable shortening, 1 cup milk

Melt chocolate with water in top of double boiler over hot water, stirring until chocolate is melted and mixture thickens. Add ½ cup sugar to mixture; cook and stir 2 minutes longer. Cool to lukewarm.

Sift flour with soda and salt. Cream shortening; gradually add 1¼ cups sugar; cream until light and fluffy. Add eggs, one at a time, beating thoroughly after each addition. Alternately add flour mixture and milk, beating after each addition until smooth. Blend in vanilla and chocolate mixture. Pour batter into three 9-inch layer pans that have been lined on bottoms with paper. Bake at 350° for 25 minutes, or until cake springs back when touched lightly. Cool in pans 10 minutes; remove from pans and cool thoroughly on racks.

Note: This cake may also be baked at 350° in the following pans lined on bottoms with paper:

A 13 × 9-inch pan for 40 to 45 minutes.

Two 9-inch square or layer pans for 30 to 35 minutes.

Two 8-inch square pans for 35 to 40 minutes.

Three 8-inch layer pans for 25 to 30 minutes.

36 muffin pans lined with paper baking cups for 25 to 30 minutes.

Opposite: Wellesley Fudge Cake with Mocha Butter Frosting and Chocolate Drizzle

MOCHA BUTTER FROSTING
(Illustrated page 89)

1 pound unsifted
   confectioners sugar
¼ cup cocoa
⅛ teaspoon salt
¼ cup butter or margarine

¼ cup vegetable shortening
⅓ cup (about) cold brewed
   Maxwell House coffee
½ teaspoon vanilla

Sift sugar with cocoa and salt. Cream butter and shortening. Gradually add part of sugar mixture, blending after each addition until light and fluffy. Add remaining sugar alternately with coffee until of right consistency to spread, beating after each addition until smooth. Blend in vanilla. Makes about 3 cups.

Chocolate Drizzle. Heat 2 squares Baker's semi-sweet chocolate with 1 tablespoon butter or margarine and 1 tablespoon corn syrup over low heat until chocolate is partially melted. Then stir rapidly until chocolate is entirely melted. Drizzle from tip of spoon in thin streams down the sides of frosted cake.

PINEAPPLE UPSIDE-DOWN CAKE

Cora says: "I bake this in a heavy iron skillet I've had for ages—just seems right for this old-fashioned favorite."

¼ cup butter or margarine
½ cup firmly packed brown
   sugar
1 can (8 oz.) sliced
   pineapple, drained
   and cut in wedges
1 cup broken pecans
   (optional)
1⅓ cups sifted cake flour

¾ cup granulated sugar
2 teaspoons Calumet
   baking powder
¼ teaspoon salt
¼ cup butter or other
   shortening
1 egg
½ cup milk
1 teaspoon vanilla

Melt ¼ cup butter in an 8-inch square pan or 8-inch oven-proof skillet. Blend in brown sugar. Remove from heat. Arrange pineapple wedges in sugar mixture, sprinkle with nuts and set aside.

Sift flour with granulated sugar, baking powder and salt. Cream ¼ cup butter. Add flour mixture, egg, milk and vanilla. Stir just until all flour is dampened; then beat vigorously 1 minute.

Pour batter over fruit mixture in pan. Bake at 350° for 50 minutes, or until cake springs back when pressed lightly. Cool in pan 5 minutes. Invert onto serving plate and let stand 1 minute before removing pan. Serve warm with whipped cream, if desired.

Peach Upside-Down Cake. Prepare Pineapple Upside-Down Cake as directed, substituting 1¼ cups well-drained sliced fresh or canned peaches for the pineapple.

SPICY HONEY-NUT CAKE

3 egg yolks	½ teaspoon grated lemon rind
¼ cup sugar	
1 teaspoon Calumet baking powder	¼ teaspoon vanilla
	1 cup walnuts, finely chopped
¼ teaspoon ground cinnamon	¾ cup Post Grape-Nuts flakes, crushed
¼ teaspoon ground cloves	3 egg whites
2 teaspoons water	½ cup honey
1 teaspoon grated orange rind	2 tablespoons water

Beat egg yolks until thick and light in color. Gradually beat in sugar, blending well. Stir in baking powder, spices, water, orange and lemon rinds, vanilla, nuts and cereal. Beat egg whites until peaks will form. Fold into cereal mixture. Pour into a greased 9-inch square pan. Bake at 350° for about 30 minutes, or until cake begins to pull away from sides of pan. Cool in pan.

Combine honey and water in saucepan; heat and stir until blended. Cool to lukewarm. Then pour over cool cake; let stand until absorbed. Cut in squares. Top with small scoops of vanilla ice cream or whipped cream, if desired. Makes 12 servings.

APPLESAUCE-RAISIN CUPCAKES

2 cups sifted cake flour	½ cup vegetable shortening,
1 cup granulated sugar	at room temperature
2 teaspoons Calumet	½ cup thick sweetened
baking powder	applesauce
¾ teaspoon salt	1 teaspoon vanilla
¼ teaspoon baking soda	2 eggs
½ teaspoon ground	½ cup thick sweetened
cinnamon	applesauce
½ teaspoon ground cloves	½ cup chopped raisins
½ teaspoon ground allspice	½ cup chopped nuts

Sift together flour, sugar, baking powder, salt, soda and spices. Stir shortening just to soften. Add flour mixture, ½ cup applesauce, the vanilla and eggs. Mix until all flour is dampened; then *beat 2 minutes* at medium speed of electric mixer or 300 vigorous strokes by hand. Add ½ cup applesauce, the raisins and nuts; *beat 1 minute* longer with mixer or 150 strokes by hand.

Pour batter into 30 muffin pans lined with paper baking cups. Bake at 350° for 30 minutes, or until cake tester inserted into center of cupcake comes out clean.

Note: This cake may also be baked in the following pans lined on bottoms with paper: a 9 x 5-inch loaf pan for 1 hour and 10 to 15 minutes; a 9-inch square pan for 45 to 50 minutes.

SEAFOAM FROSTING

2 egg whites	Dash of salt
1½ cups firmly packed	⅓ cup water
brown sugar	1 teaspoon vanilla

Combine egg whites, brown sugar, salt and water in top of double boiler. Beat with electric mixer or hand beater until thoroughly mixed, about 1 minute. Place over boiling water and beat constantly at high speed of electric mixer or with hand beater until frosting stands in stiff peaks, about 7 minutes. (Stir frosting up from bottom and sides of pan occasionally with rubber scraper.) Remove from boiling water. Pour at once into a large bowl. Add vanilla and beat until thick enough to spread, about 1 minute. Makes about 5½ cups.

Opposite: Applesauce Raisin Cupcakes with Seafoam Frosting (front), Chocolate Icebox Cake (left; recipe, p. 105), Old-Fashioned Jelly Roll (right; recipe, p. 98), and Cranberry Mince Pie (rear; recipe, p. 98)

APPLE-NUT TORTE

Cora says: "A torte rich with the taste of apples!"

⅔ cup all-purpose flour
3 teaspoons Calumet
   baking powder
½ teaspoon salt
2 eggs

1½ cups sugar
1 tablespoon vanilla
2 cups diced raw apples
1 cup chopped walnuts

Mix flour with baking powder and salt. Beat eggs until thick and light in color. Gradually beat in sugar; add vanilla. Stir in dry ingredients, apples and nuts. Spread in greased 9-inch square pan or baking dish. Bake at 350° for 45 minutes, or until golden brown. Serve warm, with cream or ice cream, if desired.

Note: Recipe may be halved, using ⅔ cup sugar; bake in greased 1-quart casserole for 35 to 40 minutes.

TRADITIONAL APPLE PIE

Cora says: "Nothing tops off a warm piece of apple pie better than a thick slice of cheddar cheese or a plump scoop of ice cream."

5 cups thinly sliced peeled
   fresh apples*
1½ tablespoons Minute
   tapioca
¾ cup sugar
¾ teaspoon ground
   cinnamon

¼ teaspoon ground nutmeg
⅛ teaspoon salt
   Pastry for two-crust
    9-inch pie
1 tablespoon butter or
   margarine

*Greening, Cortland, Rome Beauty, Wealthy or McIntosh

Combine apples, tapioca, sugar, cinnamon, nutmeg and salt. Let stand about 15 minutes. Roll out half the pastry very thin (less than ⅛ inch thick). Line a 9-inch pie pan; trim pastry at edge of rim. Roll out remaining pastry very thin. Cut several small slits or a design near center. Fill pie shell with apple mixture; dot with butter. Moisten edge of bottom crust. Place top crust over filling. Open slits to permit escape of steam. Trim top crust, letting it extend ½ inch over rim. To seal, press top and bottom crusts together on rim; then fold edge of top crust under bottom crust and flute. Bake at 425° until syrup boils with heavy bubbles that do not burst, about 55 minutes.

CHERRY PIE

Cora says: "Top this delicious old favorite with big scoops of vanilla ice cream or a stream of heavy cream for a smooth summer taste."

1½ cups sugar
4 tablespoons Minute
   tapioca
¼ teaspoon salt
4 cups pitted fresh red sour
   cherries

Pastry for two-crust
   9-inch pie
1 tablespoon butter or
   margarine

Combine sugar, tapioca and salt in saucepan; add cherries. Let stand 15 minutes.

Roll out half of pastry very thin (less than ⅛ inch thick). Line a 9-inch pie pan. Trim pastry at edge. Roll out remaining pastry very thin. Cut several small slits or a design near center. Fill bottom crust with cherry mixture. Dot with butter. Moisten edge of bottom crust. Place top crust over filling. Open slits to permit escape of steam. Trim top crust, letting it extend ½ inch over rim. To seal, press top and bottom crusts together on rim; then fold edge of top crust under bottom crust and flute. Bake at 425° for 55 minutes, or until syrup boils with heavy bubbles that do not burst. Cool before cutting.

TAPIOCA CREAM PIE

Cora says: "When fresh fruit is in season, decorate the top of this creamy pie with generous slices of your favorite."

⅓ cup sugar
3 tablespoons Minute
   tapioca
¼ teaspoon salt
3 cups milk
1 teaspoon vanilla

1 tablespoon butter or
   margarine
2 eggs, slightly beaten
1 lightly baked 9-inch pie
   shell
Ground nutmeg

Combine sugar, tapioca and salt in saucepan. Add milk and let stand 5 minutes. Cook and stir over medium heat until mixture comes to a full boil, 6 to 8 minutes. Remove from heat; add vanilla and butter. Stir into slightly beaten eggs. Pour into pie shell and sprinkle with nutmeg. Bake at 325° for 25 to 30 minutes, or until a knife inserted in center of pie comes out *almost* clean. Cool, and serve with a fruit sauce, if desired.

SHOO FLY PIE

Cora says: "Mmmm! Smooth molasses filling and crunchy crumb topping—straight from the Pennsylvania Dutch country."

2½ cups all-purpose flour
1 teaspoon Calumet
   baking powder
¾ cup sugar
   Dash of salt

¾ cup butter or margarine
1 cup molasses
1 teaspoon baking soda
1¾ cups boiling water
2 unbaked 9-inch pie shells

Mix flour, baking powder, sugar and salt in a large bowl. Cut in butter with pastry blender or two knives until crumbs are formed. Combine molasses, baking soda and boiling water, mixing well to blend. Pour about ½ cup of the liquid into each pie shell; sprinkle with about ½ cup of the crumb mixture. Continue layering, ending with crumbs. Bake at 375° for 40 to 45 minutes, or until crust is browned and a cake tester inserted in center comes out clean. Serve warm or cold.

Note: To make one 9-inch pie, use 1 cup minus 2 tablespoons boiling water and halve remaining ingredients.

STRAWBERRY-RHUBARB CRISSCROSS PIE

1¼ cups sugar
¼ cup Minute tapioca
¼ teaspoon salt
2 cups fresh strawberry
   halves
2 cups sliced fresh rhubarb

Pastry for two-crust
   9-inch pie
1 tablespoon butter or
   margarine
1 egg, slightly beaten
   (optional)

Combine sugar, tapioca, salt and fruits. Let stand about 15 minutes. Meanwhile, roll out half the pastry very thin (less than ⅛ inch thick). Line a 9-inch pie pan. Trim pastry at edge. Roll out remaining pastry very thin and cut into ½-inch strips. Fill pie shell with fruit mixture. Dot with butter. Moisten edge of bottom crust. Adjust pastry strips in lattice pattern across top of filling; press ends of strips against edge of bottom crust. Flute edge. Brush top crust with egg. Bake at 425° for 45 minutes, or until syrup boils with heavy bubbles that do not burst.

Opposite: Strawberry-Rhubarb Crisscross Pie

CRANBERRY MINCE PIE
(Illustrated page 92)

Cora says: "Here's a festive pie that combines two favorite holiday flavors."

1 cup sugar	Pastry for two-crust
¼ cup Minute tapioca	9-inch pie
½ teaspoon salt	1 tablespoon butter or
2 cups fresh cranberries	margarine
1½ cups moist mincemeat	Milk
¾ cup water	Sugar

Combine sugar, tapioca and salt in saucepan. Add cranberries, mincemeat and water. Let stand 15 minutes. Cook and stir over medium heat until mixture comes to a boil. Cool, stirring occasionally. Roll out half of pastry very thin (less than ⅛ inch thick). Line a 9-inch pie pan. Trim pastry at edge. Roll out remaining pastry very thin. Cut several small slits or a design near center. Fill bottom crust with cranberry mixture. Dot with butter. Moisten edge of bottom crust. Place top crust over filling. Open slits to permit escape of steam. Trim top crust, letting it extend ½ inch over rim. To seal, press top and bottom crust together on rim; then fold edge of top crust under bottom crust and flute. Brush top crust with milk and sprinkle with sugar. Bake at 425° for 45 to 50 minutes, or until syrup boils with heavy bubbles that do not burst. Serve warm.

Note: For pastry garnish, trim top to extend only ¼ inch over rim; roll excess dough and cut into small circles. Moisten edge of crust and press on circles, overlapping slightly.

OLD-FASHIONED JELLY ROLL
(Illustrated page 92)

¾ cup sifted cake flour	1 teaspoon vanilla
¾ teaspoon Calumet baking powder	2 tablespoons butter or margarine, melted
¼ teaspoon salt	(optional)
4 eggs, at room temperature	Confectioners sugar
¾ cup granulated sugar	1 cup tart jelly

Sift flour with baking powder and salt. Beat eggs in large bowl at high speed of electric mixer or with hand beater, adding granulated sugar gradually and beating until mixture becomes fluffy, thick and light colored, about 5 minutes. Gradually fold in flour mixture; add vanilla and butter. Pour into a 15 × 10-inch jelly roll pan which has been greased, lined on bottom with paper, and greased again. Bake at 400° for 13 minutes. Turn out onto cloth sprinkled with confectioners sugar. Quickly remove paper and trim off crisp edges. Starting with short side, roll cake with cloth. Cool on a rack about 30 minutes. Unroll. Remove cloth and spread with jelly. Roll cake again, leaving the end underneath. Sprinkle with confectioners sugar.

PEACH COBBLER

1 cup sifted all-purpose flour	2 tablespoons sugar
1 tablespoon sugar	1 tablespoon Minute tapioca
2 teaspoons Calumet baking powder	1 tablespoon lemon juice
¼ teaspoon salt	⅛ teaspoon ground nutmeg
¼ cup shortening	¼ teaspoon almond extract
⅓ cup milk	1 tablespoon butter or margarine
1 can (29 oz.) sliced peaches	

Sift flour with 1 tablespoon sugar, the baking powder and salt. Cut in shortening until mixture resembles coarse crumbs. Add milk; stir with fork until soft dough is formed. Pat or roll dough on lightly floured board until dough will fit top of 1½-quart baking dish. Cut several slits near center.

Drain peaches, measuring ¾ cup syrup. Combine measured syrup, drained peaches, 2 tablespoons sugar, the tapioca, lemon juice and nutmeg in saucepan. Let stand 5 minutes. Cook and stir until mixture comes to a full boil. Add almond extract and pour into greased 1½-quart baking dish. Dot with butter. Adjust dough on hot fruit mixture, opening slits to permit escape of steam. Bake at 400° for 25 to 30 minutes, or until top is golden brown. Makes 6 servings.

APPLE CRISP

Cora says: "A quick and easy dessert that can be baking while you eat your meal. Top each serving with a scoop of ice cream for a delicious company treat."

6 cups thinly sliced peeled apples
⅓ cup sugar
2 tablespoons butter or margarine, melted
1 teaspoon ground cinnamon
½ teaspoon salt
6 tablespoons butter or margarine
½ cup sugar
2 tablespoons all-purpose flour
3 cups Post raisin bran

Mix together apples, ⅓ cup sugar, the melted butter, cinnamon and salt. Place in a greased 8-inch square pan; set aside. Cream 6 tablespoons butter. Blend in ½ cup sugar; add flour and cereal, and crumble together. Sprinkle over apple mixture. Cover and bake at 350° for 30 minutes. Remove cover and bake 15 minutes longer, or until apples are tender. Serve warm with cream, if desired. Makes 8 servings.

INDIAN PUDDING

Cora says: "Here's a satisfying, spicy, old-time dessert the whole family will love."

3½ cups milk
½ cup yellow cornmeal
2 eggs
½ cup Log Cabin syrup
¼ cup dark molasses
1 teaspoon salt
¾ teaspoon ground cinnamon
¾ teaspoon ground ginger
2 tablespoons butter or margarine, melted

Scald 3 cups of the milk in top of double boiler. Mix remaining ½ cup milk with cornmeal. Stir into scalded milk; cook over gently boiling water for 30 minutes, stirring occasionally. Beat eggs slightly in 1½-quart baking dish; add syrup, molasses, salt, spices and butter. Gradually stir in hot cornmeal mixture. Place dish in pan of hot water, and bake at 350° for 1 hour, or until firm in center. Makes 8 to 10 servings.

Opposite: Apple Crisp

PUFF PUDDING

¼ cup butter or margarine
½ cup sugar or honey
1 teaspoon grated lemon rind
2 egg yolks
3 tablespoons lemon juice
2 tablespoons all-purpose flour
¼ cup Post Grape-Nuts brand cereal
1 cup milk
2 egg whites, stiffly beaten

Thoroughly cream butter with sugar and lemon rind. Add egg yolks and beat until light and fluffy. Blend in lemon juice, flour, cereal and milk. (Mixture will look curdled.) Fold in beaten egg whites. Pour into greased 1-quart baking dish and place in pan of hot water. Bake at 325° for 1 hour and 15 minutes, or until top springs back when lightly touched. (When done, pudding has a cake-like layer on top with custard below.) Serve warm or cold with whipped cream, if desired. Makes 6 servings.

BLUEBERRY PUDDING CAKE

⅓ cup granulated sugar
⅓ cup firmly packed brown sugar
2 tablespoons Minute tapioca
¼ teaspoon salt
¾ cup water
2 tablespoons lemon juice
1 tablespoon butter or margarine
2 cups fresh blueberries
1½ cups sifted cake flour
2 teaspoons Calumet baking powder
½ teaspoon salt
3 tablespoons butter or margarine
¾ cup granulated sugar
¾ cup milk
½ teaspoon vanilla

Combine ⅓ cup granulated sugar, the brown sugar, tapioca and ¼ teaspoon salt in saucepan. Add water and let stand 5 minutes. Cook and stir over medium heat until mixture comes to a *full* boil. Add lemon juice, 1 tablespoon butter and the blueberries. Let stand 15 minutes; stir and pour into a greased 1½-quart casserole or 8-inch square pan.

Meanwhile, sift flour with baking powder and ½ teaspoon salt. Cream 3 tablespoons butter; gradually add ¾ cup granulated sugar, beating well. Add flour mixture alternately with milk, beating after each addition until smooth. Add vanilla. Spoon batter over tapioca mixture. Bake at 375° for 50 minutes, or until cake tester inserted into center comes out clean. Serve warm. Makes 8 to 10 servings.

Molded, frozen, whipped—you'll find them all here, and they all have two things in common: they come out of the refrigerator and they're delicious. Added bonus for all of us busy cooks: you can make them ahead of time, pull them out when *you* are ready. They wait for you, not the other way 'round.

JELLIED PRUNE WHIP

1 package (3 oz.) Jell-O brand orange or lemon gelatin
¼ teaspoon salt
1 cup boiling water
¾ cup cold water
¼ teaspoon grated orange rind
¼ cup sugar
1½ cups chopped pitted cooked prunes (about 1 lb. dried prunes)

Dissolve gelatin and salt in boiling water. Add cold water and orange rind. Place bowl of gelatin in larger bowl of ice and water; stir until slightly thickened. Whip until fluffy and thick and about double in volume. Add sugar to prune pulp and fold into whipped gelatin. Pile lightly in sherbet glasses. Chill until set, at least 1 hour. Serve with custard sauce or light cream, if desired. Makes 5 cups or 8 to 10 servings.

FROSTED LIME SHERBET

1 package (3 oz.) Jell-O brand lime gelatin
Dash of salt
½ cup boiling water
½ cup sugar
2 cups milk
1 cup light cream or half and half
¼ cup lemon juice
1 teaspoon grated lemon rind

Dissolve gelatin and salt in boiling water. Add sugar and stir until dissolved. Stir in remaining ingredients. Pour into a shallow pan and freeze until partially frozen. Spoon into chilled bowl and beat with hand beater until smooth and fluffy. Pour into pan and freeze until firm, about 4 to 6 hours. Makes about 1 quart.

COFFEE PARFAITS

Cora says: " 'Parfait' means perfect, and these are—chilly and refreshing, especially after a substantial meal."

⅓ cup sugar	1 cup (about) whipped
1 teaspoon unflavored	cream
gelatin	
3 cups *hot* freshly brewed	
Maxwell House coffee	

Combine sugar and gelatin in a bowl; add hot coffee, stirring until sugar and gelatin are dissolved. Pour into an 8-inch square pan. Freeze until firm, at least 3 hours. Spoon about 1 tablespoon whipped cream into each chilled parfait glass. Shave frozen coffee mixture into fine pieces by scraping with a metal spoon. (If mixture is too firm, let stand a few minutes.) Fill glasses with shaved coffee ice. Top with remaining whipped cream. Makes 6 servings.

BUTTERSCOTCH MERINGUE PIE

Cora says: "Smooth, mellow butterscotch filling topped with light, delectable meringue peaks—this one always disappears in a flash at my house."

1 package (4-serving size)	2 egg yolks
Jell-O brand	1 baked 8-inch pie shell,
butterscotch pudding	cooled
and pie filling	2 egg whites
2 cups milk	¼ cup sugar

Combine pie filling mix and ¼ cup of the milk in saucepan. Add egg yolks and blend well; add remaining milk. Cook and stir over medium heat until mixture comes to a *full* boil. Remove from heat. Cool 5 minutes, stirring twice. Pour into baked pie shell. Let stand at room temperature for 30 minutes.

Beat egg whites until foamy throughout. Gradually beat in sugar and continue beating until mixture will form stiff shiny peaks. Spread evenly over pie filling. Bake at 425° for 5 to 10 minutes, or until meringue is lightly browned. Cool to room temperature before cutting.

CHOCOLATE ICEBOX CAKE

(Illustrated page 92)

12 ladyfingers, split
1 package (4 oz.) Baker's German's sweet chocolate
1½ tablespoons water
1 egg yolk

1 tablespoon confectioners sugar
1 cup prepared or thawed whipped topping
1 egg white, stiffly beaten

Line an 8 × 4-inch loaf pan with wax paper. Place 6 ladyfingers on bottom of pan; set aside 6 for the top. Cut remaining ladyfingers in half and place, cut side up, around sides of pan. Melt chocolate over very low heat; blend in water. Remove from heat and add egg yolk, beating vigorously until smooth. Blend in sugar; cool. Fold in whipped topping and beaten egg white. Pour into pan and top with reserved ladyfingers. Chill overnight. Unmold and remove paper. Garnish with additional whipped topping, if desired. Makes 4 or 5 servings.

CREAMY RICE PUDDING

Cora says: "This creamy mixture is rich with egg yolks, milk and cream — always brings back happy memories."

1 quart milk
⅔ cup uncooked long grain rice
1 teaspoon salt
¼ teaspoon ground nutmeg

1½ teaspoons vanilla
4 egg yolks
½ cup sugar
½ cup light cream or half and half

Combine milk, rice, salt, nutmeg and vanilla in top of large double boiler. Cover and cook over boiling water, stirring occasionally, 45 minutes, or until liquid is almost absorbed. Meanwhile, combine egg yolks, sugar and cream; beat well with a wire whip. Remove rice mixture from heat. Very gradually add egg yolk mixture to rice, stirring rapidly. Then bring to a boil over *low* heat (not over boiling water), stirring constantly. Pour into a heatproof bowl, place plastic wrap directly on surface of pudding and chill thoroughly, about 4 hours. Makes about 5 cups or 8 to 10 servings.

BAKED APPLES SUPREME

Cora says: "An old favorite, nicely sparked with raspberry jam."

1 cup water	3 large baking apples
½ cup sugar	2 to 4 tablespoons red
2 teaspoons lemon juice	raspberry jam

Combine water and sugar in saucepan. Bring to a boil and boil 5 minutes; add lemon juice. Meanwhile, halve apples horizontally and remove cores, without cutting completely through apples. Fill centers with jam and place in shallow baking dish. Pour syrup over apples, cover and bake at 400° for 30 minutes, or until tender. Place apples in individual serving dishes. Boil syrup, if necessary, until slightly thickened; pour over apples, and chill. Makes 6 servings.

COFFEE JELLY
(Illustrated page 108)

Cora says: "Double the good taste of this dessert by serving it with lots of steaming coffee."

1 envelope unflavored	⅛ teaspoon salt
gelatin	2 cups brewed Maxwell
⅓ cup sugar	House coffee

Combine gelatin, sugar and salt. Bring coffee just to a boil. Pour coffee over gelatin mixture, stirring until dissolved. Pour into individual molds. Chill until firm. Unmold. Garnish with whipped cream or topping, flavored with grated orange rind, if desired, and rosettes of curled orange rind. Makes 2 cups or 4 servings.

Note: Recipe may be tripled, using 4 cups brewed coffee and 1¼ cups water. Chill in a 6-cup mold.

CREAM PUFFS

Cora says: "If you think cream puffs are hard to make, you haven't really tried. The secret of their goodness is in adding the eggs one at a time and beating well—that is important."

¾ cup vegetable shortening
1¼ cups boiling water
1½ cups all-purpose flour

6 eggs
Vanilla ice cream
Regal Chocolate Sauce

Melt shortening in boiling water. Stir in flour all at once; then cook and stir until mixture thickens and leaves sides of pan, forming a smooth, compact ball. Remove from heat. Beat in eggs one at a time, blending well after each addition; continue beating after last addition until mixture is satiny and breaks off when spoon is raised. Drop by heaping tablespoonfuls onto ungreased baking sheets. Bake at 400° for 35 to 40 minutes, or until golden brown. Remove from baking sheets and cool on racks. Cut off tops, spoon in ice cream and replace tops. Top with Regal Chocolate Sauce and serve at once. Makes 24.

Note: Unfilled cooled, baked puffs may be wrapped in airtight bags or other containers and stored in freezer. Fill without thawing; the thin shell will thaw quickly after being filled and can be served almost immediately.

REGAL CHOCOLATE SAUCE

2 squares Baker's
    unsweetened
    chocolate
6 tablespoons water
½ cup sugar

Dash of salt
3 tablespoons butter or
    margarine
¼ teaspoon vanilla

Heat chocolate and water in saucepan over low heat, stirring constantly until blended. Add sugar and salt. Cook and stir until sugar is dissolved, and mixture is very slightly thickened and smooth, about 5 minutes. Remove from heat; add butter and vanilla. Makes about 1 cup sauce.

I call these "extras"—and what would life be without them? If you have a "sweet-snitcher" around—someone who just can't resist a few between-meal goodies—here's the answer. A full cookie jar or a pan of homemade fudge just spells heaven to a youngster. To most grown-ups, too!

MINCEMEAT SURPRISES
(Illustrated page 113)

Cora says: "These miniature filled cookies are a delight to adults as well as children."

3½ cups sifted cake flour	1 egg
2 teaspoons Calumet baking powder	2 tablespoons milk
½ teaspoon salt	1 teaspoon vanilla
¾ cup butter or other shortening	1 cup moist mincemeat
1¼ cups firmly packed brown sugar	¼ cup firmly packed brown sugar
	½ teaspoon rum flavoring

Sift flour with baking powder and salt. Cream shortening. Gradually add 1¼ cups brown sugar; continue beating until light and fluffy. Add egg and beat well. Then add flour mixture alternately with milk, beating well after each addition. Blend in vanilla. Chill until firm.

Mix mincemeat with brown sugar and rum flavoring. Using a small amount of the chilled dough at a time, roll ⅛ inch thick on floured board. (Keep remaining dough chilled.) Cut with floured 2½-inch cutter or cut in 2½-inch squares; cut a small hole or star in center of half the circles. Place whole circles on ungreased baking sheet, and spread to ¼ inch of the edge with 1 teaspoon mincemeat. Top with remaining cut circles, pressing edges to seal well. Bake at 425° for 8 to 10 minutes, or until lightly browned. Sprinkle with confectioners sugar, if desired. Makes about 3½ dozen cookies.

Opposite: Coffee Jelly (recipe, p. 106)

CRISP HERMITS

Cora says: "Spicy and loaded with raisins, these have been enjoyed in my family for generations."

1¾ cups cake flour
½ cup granulated sugar
2 teaspoons Calumet
   baking powder
¼ teaspoon salt
1 teaspoon ground
   cinnamon
1 teaspoon ground mace

½ cup firmly packed brown
   sugar
¼ cup milk
½ cup butter or other
   shortening
2 eggs, well beaten
1 cup raisins
½ cup chopped nuts

Mix flour with granulated sugar, baking powder, salt and spices. Combine brown sugar and milk. Cream shortening. Add flour mixture, brown sugar mixture and eggs. Stir until all flour is dampened; then beat vigorously 1 minute. Mix in raisins and nuts. Drop from teaspoon onto greased baking sheets. Bake at 350° for 15 minutes, or until lightly browned. Store in tightly covered container. Makes about 3½ dozen.

OLD-FASHIONED SUGAR COOKIES

3½ cups sifted all-purpose
   flour
2½ teaspoons Calumet
   baking powder
¾ teaspoon salt

½ cup butter or margarine
½ cup shortening
1⅔ cups sugar
2 eggs
3 teaspoons vanilla

Sift flour with baking powder and salt. Cream butter and shortening together. Gradually add sugar and beat until light and fluffy. Add eggs, one at a time, beating thoroughly after each addition. Add vanilla. Gradually add the flour mixture, blending thoroughly after each addition. Roll dough into small balls, about 1 inch in diameter, and place about 2 inches apart on greased cookie sheets. Using a flat-bottomed glass or a jar cover, buttered and dipped in granulated sugar, press cookies to measure about 3 inches in diameter, ⅛ inch thick. Bake at 400° for 6 to 8 minutes or until edges are lightly browned. Makes about 5 dozen.

JUMBO RAISIN COOKIES

2 cups raisins
1 cup water
4 cups sifted all-purpose
  flour
1 teaspoon Calumet
  baking powder
1 teaspoon baking soda
1 teaspoon salt
½ teaspoon ground
  cinnamon

½ teaspoon ground nutmeg
1 cup butter or shortening,
  or ½ cup of each
1¾ cups sugar
2 eggs, slightly beaten
1 teaspoon vanilla
½ cup chopped nuts

Place raisins and water in a saucepan; bring to a boil and boil about 3 minutes. Set aside to cool; do not drain.

Sift flour with baking powder, soda, salt and spices. Cream butter. Gradually beat in sugar, creaming well after each addition. Add eggs and vanilla; mix well. Stir in the raisins with liquid. Gradually add the flour mixture, blending thoroughly after each addition. Stir in nuts. Drop from tablespoon, about 2 inches apart, on greased baking sheets. Bake at 375° for 12 to 15 minutes. Makes about 3½ dozen.

OATMEAL DROP COOKIES
(Illustrated page 113)

1¾ cups all-purpose flour
1 teaspoon Calumet
  baking powder
1 teaspoon salt
1 teaspoon ground
  cinnamon
1 cup shortening

2 eggs
2 cups uncooked
  old-fashioned oats
1¼ cups Log Cabin syrup
1 cup raisins
½ cup chopped nuts

Mix flour with baking powder, salt and cinnamon. Cream shortening. Add eggs one at a time, beating thoroughly after each addition. (Batter may appear curdled.) Add flour mixture and oats alternately with syrup, mixing well. Stir in raisins and nuts. Drop from teaspoon onto ungreased baking sheets. Bake at 375° for 12 to 15 minutes, or until lightly browned. Makes about 5 dozen.

Note: For larger cookies, drop by heaping teaspoonfuls; makes about 1½ dozen.

CHOCOLATE-DIPPED COOKIES
(Illustrated page 124)

2¼ cups sifted all-purpose
    flour
1½ tablespoons Maxwell
    House instant coffee
½ teaspoon salt
¼ teaspoon Calumet
    baking powder

1 cup butter or margarine
¾ cup sugar
1 egg
1 teaspoon vanilla
    Baker's semi-sweet
      chocolate, melted
    Finely chopped walnuts

Sift flour with instant coffee, salt and baking powder. Cream butter. Gradually add sugar, beating until light and fluffy. Add egg and vanilla; beat well. Gradually add flour mixture, beating well after each addition. Drop from teaspoon onto ungreased baking sheets. Bake at 375° for 10 to 12 minutes. Cool thoroughly. Dip half of each cookie into melted chocolate and sprinkle with nuts. Makes about 4 dozen.

Note: Dough may be pressed from cookie press with star shape to form 3-inch logs. Makes about 8 dozen.

CHOCOLATE-NUT COOKIES

3 squares Baker's
    semi-sweet chocolate
1½ cups sifted all-purpose
    flour
¾ teaspoon Calumet
    baking powder
¼ teaspoon salt
⅓ cup milk

½ teaspoon vanilla
½ cup shortening
1 cup firmly packed brown
    sugar
1 egg
1 cup chopped raisins
1 cup chopped walnuts

Partially melt chocolate in saucepan over very low heat. Remove from heat and stir rapidly until entirely melted. Sift flour with baking powder and salt. Combine milk and vanilla. Cream shortening; gradually add sugar, beating until light and fluffy. Blend in egg and chocolate. Add flour mixture alternately with milk mixture, blending well after each addition. Stir in raisins and walnuts. Drop from teaspoon onto greased baking sheets. Bake at 375° for 10 to 12 minutes. Makes 5 dozen.

Note: For larger cookies, drop by heaping teaspoonfuls. Makes about 2 dozen.

Opposite: Mincemeat Surprises (front; recipe, p. 109), Oatmeal Drop Cookies (left; recipe, p. 111), and Chocolate-Nut Cookies (right)

LINZER COOKIES

½ cup butter or margarine
¼ cup granulated sugar
1 egg
1 teaspoon vanilla
¼ teaspoon almond extract
½ teaspoon salt
1¼ cups sifted cake flour
¾ cup fine dry bread crumbs
1 cup finely ground blanched almonds
Confectioners sugar
¾ cup red raspberry or peach jam

Cream butter. Gradually blend in granulated sugar, creaming well after each addition. Add egg; beat well. Stir in vanilla, almond extract and salt. Add flour, bread crumbs and almonds; mix well.

Roll dough very thin (less than ⅛ inch thick) on board that has been lightly floured, then sprinkled with confectioners sugar. Cut with a 2-inch scalloped cookie cutter. Cut a hole in the center of half of the cookies with a 1-inch round cookie cutter. Bake on greased baking sheets at 375° for about 7 minutes, or until browned. Remove immediately from sheets and cool on racks. Sprinkle confectioners sugar over cookie rings. Spread jam over bottoms of the whole cookies. Top each with a cookie ring; press together lightly. Makes 1½ dozen filled cookies.

Note: For larger cookies, cut with 3½-inch scalloped cutter and 1½-inch round cutter. Makes 1 dozen.

CHOCOLATE PINWHEELS

Cora says: "The promise of a few cookies and a tall glass of milk will bring any child straight home from school!"

2¼ cups sifted all-purpose flour
1 teaspoon Calumet baking powder
½ teaspoon salt
⅔ cup butter or other shortening
1 cup sugar
1 egg
1 teaspoon vanilla
2 squares Baker's unsweetened chocolate, melted

Sift flour with baking powder and salt. Cream butter; gradually add sugar, beating until light and fluffy. Add egg and vanilla;

beat well. Add flour mixture, a small amount at a time, mixing well after each addition. Divide dough in half; blend chocolate into one half. Roll chocolate and plain dough separately between wax paper into 12 × 8-inch rectangles. Remove top sheets of paper. Invert plain dough onto chocolate dough and remove remaining paper. Roll as for jelly roll; wrap in wax paper. Chill until firm, at least 3 hours in refrigerator or 1 hour in freezer. Cut in ¼-inch slices. Place on ungreased baking sheets. Bake at 375° for about 10 minutes or until cookies just begin to brown around edges. Makes about 4½ dozen.

CHOCOLATE FUDGE

Cora says: "Lots of my happy memories seem to revolve around making fudge. No wonder—it's a satisfying project to make, even better to eat."

4 squares Baker's unsweetened chocolate	4 cups sugar
	⅛ teaspoon salt
	¼ cup butter or margarine
1½ cups milk	2 teaspoons vanilla

Place chocolate and milk in heavy saucepan. Cook and stir over very low heat until mixture is smooth, well blended and slightly thickened. Add sugar and salt; stir over medium heat until sugar is dissolved and mixture boils. Continue boiling over medium heat, without stirring, until small amount of mixture forms a soft ball which can be rolled with the fingers into a definite shape in cold water (or to a temperature of 234°). Remove from heat; add butter and vanilla. *Do not stir.* Cool to lukewarm (110°). Beat until mixture begins to lose its gloss and holds its shape. Pour at once into buttered 8-inch square pan. Cool until set; then cut into squares. Let stand in pan until firm. Store in covered container. Makes about 2 pounds or about 3 dozen pieces.

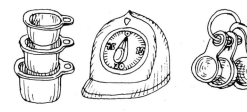

STAR ATTRACTIONS
THROUGH THE DAY

I call coffee the all-day, everyday drink. You probably think of it that way, too. You've always known coffee was a delicious, satisfying brew, but I bet you never realized it was so versatile. Take a look at these recipes—they range from Soda Fountain Punch to Irish Coffee. Some could take the place of dessert, some would be perfect along with dessert. For a double taste sensation, serve a coffee beverage along with a coffee dessert—maybe Spiced Brazilian Chocolate with Coffee Jelly. Even more to the point, keep in mind that these beverage recipes are good just about any time of the day. The Hot Chocolate is just the ticket when a group comes to your place after an hour or two of ice skating. Or you could serve Coffee Chocolaccino at a morning kaffeeklatsch or afternoon break. Unwind at the end of the day with Coffee Neapolitan. Cool off on a sizzling summer day with Iced Spiced Coffee. But you don't need suggestions from me. Go to it! No wonder we Americans love our coffee—it's great in food, with food or just by itself. Hurray for coffee!

Nothing beats a frosty coffee-flavored beverage on a hot day when you're wilted and frazzled. These are so good they stand by themselves, but most can double as dessert, too. Serve them with festive straws and long-handled spoons and create an instant party.

ICED COFFEE

Freshly brewed Maxwell House coffee
Ice cubes

Cream and sugar (optional)

For each glass of iced coffee desired, brew coffee using 2 level tablespoons coffee and ¾ measuring cup (6 fl. oz.) cold water. *Use more or less to suit your taste.* Pour hot coffee over ice cubes in tall glasses. Serve immediately with cream and sugar.

COFFEE ICE CUBES *(Illustrated page 121)*

3 cups (about) brewed Maxwell House regular grind or Electra-Perk coffee, cooled

Pour coffee into freezer tray. Freeze until firm, at least 5 hours. If used with cold coffee, makes enough cubes for eight 12-ounce glasses; with hot coffee, enough for five 12-ounce glasses.

COFFEE FROSTED *(Illustrated page 121)*

Cora says: "Serve this instead of dessert some night—or for a dessert and coffee party."

2 cups brewed Maxwell House coffee, chilled
1 pint vanilla, coffee or chocolate ice cream

Coffee Ice Cubes (above)

Combine coffee and ice cream in a bowl and beat until blended and thick. Serve immediately over Coffee Ice Cubes in tall glasses. Makes 3⅔ cups or 3 or 4 servings.

ICED SPICED COFFEE *(Illustrated page 121)*

½ cup Maxwell House
   regular grind or
   Electra-Perk coffee
3 cups water
¼ cup sugar

2 sticks cinnamon
6 whole cloves
6 whole allspice
   Coffee Ice Cubes (see
   page 117)

Place coffee and water in percolator. Percolate gently 5 to 8 minutes, or until desired strength. Remove basket. Add sugar and spices; stir until sugar is dissolved. Cover, let steep 30 minutes and strain. Pour over ice cubes in tall glasses. Serve with cream, if desired. Makes 3 cups or 4 servings.

SODA FOUNTAIN PUNCH

Cora says: "What do young folks love more than ice cream sodas? This one would appease the appetite of any mid-afternoon snacker."

3 cups brewed Maxwell
   House coffee, chilled
⅓ cup sugar
2 bottles (7 fl. oz. each)
   club soda, chilled

2 cups (1 pt.) vanilla ice
   cream, softened

Combine coffee and sugar in a large bowl; stir until sugar is dissolved. Add club soda; then stir in softened ice cream. Sprinkle with ground cinnamon, if desired. Makes about 7 cups or 14 servings in punch cups or 6 to 8 servings in tall glasses.

CHOCOLATE SYRUP

Cora says: "This rich syrup can be added to warm or cold milk for a perfect chocolate drink or used as is over ice cream or cake."

4 squares Baker's
   unsweetened
   chocolate
1¼ cups hot water

1 cup sugar
¼ teaspoon salt
½ teaspoon vanilla

Heat chocolate with water in heavy saucepan over low heat, stirring constantly, until thick, well blended and very smooth. Add sugar and salt. Bring to a boil and boil 2 minutes, stirring constantly. Remove from heat; add vanilla and cool. Store in refrigerator in tightly covered jar. Makes 2 cups.

BLACK AND WHITE SODA

2 tablespoons Chocolate
   Syrup (see page 118)
½ cup cold milk

½ cup cold club soda
Vanilla ice cream

Pour syrup into a tall glass. Stir in milk, blending well. Add club soda and top with a scoop of ice cream. Serve at once. Makes 1 serving.

ICE CREAM FLOAT

2 tablespoons Chocolate
   Syrup (see page 118)
1 cup milk

1 scoop chocolate, vanilla
   or coffee ice cream

Measure syrup into shaker or jar with tightly fitting cover. Gradually stir in milk. Shake well until foamy. Pour into tall glass. Add ice cream. Makes 1 serving.

SWITCHEL

Cora says: "The unusual spicy-sweet flavor is a treat—bet folks can't guess what's in this punch."

1 cup Log Cabin syrup
¾ cup vinegar
⅓ cup molasses

¾ teaspoon ground ginger
2 quarts cold water

Combine syrup, vinegar, molasses and ginger; stir until well blended. Add water and chill well. Makes 2½ quarts or fifteen 5-ounce servings.

PARTY FRUIT PUNCH

Cora says: "This punch is perfect for a child's party—the adults won't mind drinking it either."

2 quarts water
2 cups sugar
1 can (20 oz.) crushed
   pineapple
3 cups pineapple juice
2 cups lemon juice (about
   12 lemons)

2 bottles (28 fl. oz. each)
   club soda, chilled
Maraschino cherries
Orange and lemon slices
Crushed ice

Combine water and sugar in a large saucepan. Bring to a boil and boil 10 minutes; cool. Combine syrup, pineapple with juice, pineapple and lemon juices in a large punch bowl. Just before serving, add soda. Garnish with cherries and orange and lemon slices. Serve over crushed ice or with scoops of orange sherbet, if desired. Makes 5 quarts or 40 servings.

FRUIT SHRUB COOLER

Cora says: "With or without the sherbet, this three-fruit punch is bound to cool—and please."

1 quart orange juice
2 cups pineapple juice

3 tablespoons lemon juice
1 pint orange sherbet

Combine orange, pineapple and lemon juices in a large pitcher or punch bowl. Chill well. Just before serving, add sherbet by spoonfuls, or pour over scoops of sherbet in individual glasses or punch cups. Makes about 1½ quarts without sherbet or 12 to 15 servings.

Opposite: Fruit Shrub Cooler (front), Iced Spiced Coffee (left; recipe, p. 118), Coffee Frosted (right; recipe, p. 117), and Coffee Ice Cubes (recipe, p. 117)

Warm the Cockles of Your Heart

You just feel better after some good hot coffee on a cold day. The rich flavor of coffee stands up to other full-bodied flavors like chocolate or spices. Combination's terrific!

MULLED CIDER

Cora says: "Here's a perfect drink for the youngsters on a nippy fall day, for teens after the game or ice skating party —it just smells like autumn."

4 cups apple cider
1 teaspoon whole allspice
8 whole cloves
1 stick cinnamon, broken in pieces

Place cider and spices in saucepan. Bring just to a boil; strain. Serve hot or cooled. Makes about 4 cups or 6 servings.

SPICY PUNCH

Cora says: "Here's another drink that tastes just like fall and a blazing hearth fire—serve it warm or chilled and pretty it up with a cinnamon stick stirrer."

4 cups apple juice or cider
4 cups cranberry juice cocktail
¼ teaspoon ground cinnamon
⅛ teaspoon ground nutmeg
⅛ teaspoon ground cloves

Combine apple juice, cranberry juice cocktail and the spices in saucepan, and bring just to a boil. Serve hot in punch cups or mugs, or chill and serve over crushed ice. Makes 2 quarts or 16 servings.

COFFEE NEAPOLITAN

2 tablespoons Maxwell House instant coffee
2 cups hot brewed Maxwell House coffee
2 tablespoons cognac brandy
Sugar

Dissolve instant coffee in the brewed coffee. Place 1½ teaspoons brandy in each of 4 whiskey sour glasses and fill with
hot coffee. Add sugar; top with whipped cream and sprinkle
with cinnamon, if desired. Serve at once. Makes 4 servings.

IRISH COFFEE

Cora says: "You don't have to be Irish to enjoy this famous after-dinner drink."

2 tablespoons Maxwell
House instant coffee
2 cups hot brewed Maxwell
House coffee

2 to 3 ounces Irish whisky
4 teaspoons sugar

Dissolve instant coffee in the brewed coffee; stir in whisky and sugar. Pour into large goblets or stemmed coffee cups. Top with whipped cream, if desired.

SPICED BRAZILIAN CHOCOLATE

Cora says: "This drink offers the delicious taste of mocha with added spices."

1 or 2 squares Baker's
unsweetened
chocolate
2 cups hot brewed Maxwell
House coffee
½ cup sugar

1 teaspoon ground
cinnamon
Dash of ground allspice
Dash of salt
1½ cups milk
1½ teaspoons vanilla

Place chocolate and coffee in saucepan. Stir over low heat until chocolate is melted and mixture is smooth. Bring to a boil; reduce heat and simmer gently 2 minutes, stirring constantly. Add sugar, spices and salt. Gradually stir in milk. Heat thoroughly, stirring occasionally. (If necessary, beat with hand beater to blend completely.) Remove from heat; add vanilla. Pour into cups. Top with whipped cream, if desired, and serve immediately. Makes 3¾ cups or 6 servings.

HOT CHOCOLATE

Cora says: "There's nothing simpler or tastier than hot chocolate—and this recipe is easily doubled to serve a crowd."

2 cups Chocolate Syrup (see page 118)   3 quarts hot milk

Combine syrup and milk, blending well. Makes about 3½ quarts or 18 servings.

COFFEE CHOCOLACCINO

Cora says: "Here's another mocha-flavored drink that's perfect for company."

2 tablespoons Maxwell House instant coffee   1½ tablespoons sugar
2 cups hot brewed Maxwell House coffee   1½ tablespoons Chocolate Syrup (see page 118)

Dissolve instant coffee in the brewed coffee. Add sugar and syrup. Serve hot in demitasse cups. Top with whipped cream and shaved sweet chocolate, if desired. Makes 2 cups or 6 demitasse servings.

Opposite: Coffee Chocolaccino and Chocolate-Dipped Cookies (recipe, p. 112)

Index